Green Claims

A consumer investigation into marketing claims
about the environment

By the National Consumer Council

Published by the National Consumer Council

20 Grosvenor Gardens London   SW1W 0DH

Telephone/Minicom 0171 730 3469 Fax 0171 730 0191

March 1996 PD 07/D5/96

ISBN 1 899581 30 8

About the National Consumer Council

The independent voice of consumers in the UK

It is the National Consumer Council's job to make sure the consumer voice is heard and heeded by all those whose decisions affect consumers day by day. We speak up for the consumers of public and professional services just as much as for shoppers in high streets and supermarkets. We take a special interest in vital household services like water and fuel where competition, and therefore consumer choice, is very limited. And we have a special brief to represent vulnerable consumers who are least able to make their voices heard.

The Council was set up by government in 1975 and is largely funded by the Department of Trade and Industry.

The consumer agenda

To get a better deal for consumers, we carry out research, we formulate policies, we campaign for change, and we support other consumer representatives.

Quality and value for money in the goods and services consumers use or buy every day are central to all our work. When we are investigating the consumer interest in any product or service, we focus on seven key tests - access, choice, safety, information, equity, redress and representation.

For more information

Please send for the latest issue of the **NCC Bulletin** with up-to-date news about our publications, policies and campaigns.

Every year the Council publishes a wide range of research reports, policy papers and handbooks. Please turn to page 215 for a selection of recent titles.

For more information, please don't hesitate to contact us:

National Consumer Council, 20 Grosvenor Gardens, London SW1W ODH
Telephone 0171 730 3469
Fax 0171 730 0191
Minicom 0171 730 3469

Contents

Acknowledgements

The work on which this report is based was commissioned by the Department of the Environment and the Department of Trade and Industry. It was written by Teresa Smallbone, a research consultant, with help from Marcella Sutcliffe. The draft was approved by the Council of the National Consumer Council and submitted to the government departments in December 1995.

1. An executive summary and recommendations

Information is essential to consumer choice - and to consumers' power to influence markets. People need truthful, reliable, relevant information about the goods and services on sale before they decide which ones are right for them.

This is a report about one particular category of consumer information - the marketing claims that appear on labels, packaging and advertisements about the environmental benefits of products. The Department of the Environment and the Department of Trade and Industry asked the National Consumer Council to undertake the research in response to public concern that some of the claims made by manufacturers and retailers about the environmental impact of their products and services were confusing or misleading.

Our work has included extensive research among groups of shoppers, a survey of the claims made on products currently on sale across the country, wide consultation with retailers, advertisers, environmental organisations, trade associations and manufacturers of consumer products, a literature review and a background paper commissioned from a legal academic. As far as we are aware it is the most comprehensive study of the subject ever undertaken.

Our findings

Our research shows that large numbers of products are being marketed with various claims about their impact on the environment or about their superior environmental credentials. Most environmental claims appear on products or their packaging (or both). They are scattered across a wide range of products (see chapter 3) and are also still being made, though far less frequently, in advertisements. Many of the claims made on products are unverifiable, and/or vague, woolly, specious or misleading (chapter 4). Most are accompanied by a bewildering range of logos and symbols.

When asked for their views on these claims during our market research, shoppers expressed scepticism about the truth of claims, confusion about what exactly was being claimed, and ignorance about their effect. This level of confusion and ignorance was almost as pronounced among the minority of 'green shoppers' (who professed to make a point of reading environmental information on packaging, and planning their purchases accordingly), as it was among those who were more representative of the general population (and did not make a habit of doing this). Overall, we were struck by the low level of knowledge about environmental issues in general, and believe there is a need for a co-ordinated, coherent government information campaign to remedy this situation.

Whether shoppers did, or did not, look at the environmental information and claims on products, they were united in wanting that information, in expecting it to achieve high standards of accuracy, clarity and truthfulness, in hoping that it was regulated or would be regulated in some way, and in criticising the way in which it was currently presented.

The evidence from our survey of the environmental claims currently being made shows that many are confusing, a fairly large proportion are misleading or potentially so, and a few are downright dishonest. By far the bulk of the confusing and misleading claims we found were attached to products. We have described these as *on-pack* or *product* claims in our report, to distinguish them from claims in advertisements. The distinction is, however, an artificial one. In the real world of marketing, labels and claims carried on products or their packaging generally form part of integrated marketing campaigns, of which the product design, its name, appearance and the messages on it are but one part. Unfortunately, the current regulation of marketing and advertising claims perpetuates this artificial distinction.

The current codes of practice on advertising seem to provide adequate controls on misleading environmental claims made in advertisements. Though there is a slight discrepancy between the broadcast and non-broadcast advertising codes on environmental claims (chapter 8), in practice there seems to be little difference in the way the various bodies involved have dealt with claims. The strength of these controls is that they require advertisers to be in a position to substantiate claims and, when in doubt, this evidence is subjected to expert examination. Adjudication of complaints is cheap and effective and leads to the amendment or withdrawal of the advertisement if the complaint is upheld, and to publication of the results whatever the outcome. There is very little recourse to statutory (civil law) back-up to enforce rulings. The codes can also be amended fairly readily if new abuses come to light (chapter 7).

In contrast, the statutory controls on product descriptions, through the Trade Descriptions Act 1968, do not appear to be operating well in connection with environmental claims (chapters 7 and 8). We have found very few examples of successful prosecutions, and there is some doubt about the legal basis for some of these. While we believe the Act is an effective means of policing many other types of claim, we have come to the conclusion that the majority of environmental claims on products are not susceptible to control by this means and so escape regulation altogether. The main reason for this is that most environmental claims on products are not verifiable by analysis or testing of the product: they may use terms which lack accepted or standard definitions, or employ extravagant language to mask the emptiness of the claim being made (chapter 4).

Our conclusions

As a result of the evidence we collected, we have come to the conclusion that regulation of on-product environmental claims needs to be substantially improved. In chapter 11 we examine in detail various options for dealing with misleading claims, including some which would require new legislation and some which would not. We have looked at voluntary schemes such as certification, voluntary standards and approvals schemes (chapter 9) but have come to the conclusion that at present, however well-intentioned, they just add another source of possibly contradictory information to a confusing situation.

In our view, the government needs to take action to tackle the issue. It is wrong for consumers to be deceived by false claims on products, and wrong that the claims are not being regulated properly. We also take the view that the use of misleading environmental claims undermines national policy objectives in the environmental field, which are to encourage consumers to buy more fuel-efficient, less environmentally harmful products. Since consumers use the marketing information on and with products to help them choose which to buy, they have the right to expect such information to be truthful and unambiguous.

Our recommendations

The National Consumer Council recommends that the government should take specific action to protect consumers from false and misleading environmental claims. We have identified four possible options for change.

Option one: amend the Trade Descriptions Act 1968 in certain crucial respects, but leave enforcement much as it is now.

Although we believe this would be an improvement on the current situation, we do not think the legislation is sufficiently flexible, or can be amended readily, to deal with the worst types of environmental claim without serious implications for other types of product claim.

Option two: introduce a separate Environmental Claims Act which, among other things, would require those making environmental claims to be able to substantiate them.

We believe this would be effective, but there is also likely to be a case for extending such protection to other product claims, some of which may be equally troublesome to consumers.

Option three: establish a mechanism whereby the existing, largely self-regulatory, system of controls on advertising could be extended to cover environmental claims on products.

In many ways this would be the best solution. It would extend a system which we believe is currently working well for environmental advertising claims and end the disparity of treatment between product and advertising claims, while producing negotiated solutions and a requirement that all claims be capable of substantiation. However, we accept the Advertising Standards Authority's points that they could not take on the monitoring and adjudication of environmental claims on products in isolation from all other product claims, and that it is difficult to see how this could be funded.

Option four: alter part III of the Fair Trading Act 1973, along the lines the Office of Fair Trading has proposed and the Department of Trade and Industry has already twice consulted on. The proposed new section of the Act would include an illustrative list of deceptive business practices, including misleading claims, together with provision for a code of practice on environmental claims that would have statutory backing.

Overall, given the drawbacks to the other options, this seems to us to be the most attractive option. A code of practice would give flexibility and would require those making claims to be able to substantiate them and could give guidance on what was and was not acceptable. It would be drawn up and policed to a great extent by negotiation, while providing for civil action against miscreants. An additional merit would be that it should also be possible to introduce codes of practice to deal with other types of claim where law enforcement is a problem, such as nutrition, animal welfare and ethical claims.

2. About our research

The National Consumer Council's approach to the provision of goods or services focuses on the central importance of consumers' freedom of choice when deciding what to buy, and the power this gives consumers to influence markets. For freedom of choice to be effective it must be informed. And consumers must be in a position to understand and to assimilate the information easily. Their freedom of choice is restricted if they are given inadequate, inaccurate or misleading information.

So the provision of information is something we emphasise in all our work, and which underpinned our research for this project. Consumer information must be meaningful and truthful, and written in plain English. It must not be misleading, or made false by what is omitted. It must allow easy comparisons between products. And it should be possible to read about a product's positive qualities and believe what it says.

It is common for consumers to claim that they are not influenced by advertising and marketing claims, but advertisers themselves know that consumers derive much of their information about products from advertisements. This is why the National Consumer Council has carried out a great deal of work in the last twenty years on labelling, and marketing and advertising claims.

In response to our brief from the Department of the Environment and Department of Trade and Industry, we directed our research on environmental claims into five main areas. (The full terms of the review brief are in appendix 7.) We began with a wide-ranging review of all the literature we could find on the subject, paying particular attention to research on consumers' shopping habits and into their attitudes towards environmental claims. Much of the available research dated from the late 1980s and early 1990s, the period when interest in environmental issues was at its peak. In market research terms, it was therefore fairly old, though it did provide some useful insights.

The literature review

A survey of public opinion, the results of which were published in *Which?* in January 1990, revealed that 60 per cent of those questioned had seen environmental product information on labels on their last shopping trip, nearly 60 per cent had bought a product with such a label on it on their last shopping trip, and over half of those shown such a label thought that it was officially approved.

Further evidence of widespread 'green' shopping was provided by a MORI poll, commissioned by the Department of the Environment, in June 1992. People were asked questions about the impact of environmental concerns on their shopping habits. On all counts, the impact was surprisingly high, which helps to explain why manufacturers at that time were so keen to provide information on the environmental qualities of their products. Over half the sample in this 1992 survey thought that 'environmentally friendly' brands were more expensive than conventional products, and only 40 per cent that they worked as well as products not claiming to be 'green'.

Data presented by Nielsen at a CBI conference in January 1993, which matched public attitudes with figures on supermarket sales, revealed that two-thirds of those surveyed would be prepared to pay a bit more for green products.

A continuing consumer commitment to environmentally influenced purchasing was shown in surveys by MORI and Mintel published in 1994. These could also be set against the background of a continuing high level of consumer concern about the environment in the context of other issues such as the economy and unemployment, demonstrated by some polling carried out for the Department of the Environment [NOP, *Public Attitudes to the Environment*, July-August 1993].

In the MORI study people were asked to select from a list of 'green activities' in which they might have participated in the last year or two [MORI, *Annual Survey of British Green Activism*, 1994]. In answer to the question, 'Which if any of these things have you done in the last 12 months as a result of concern for the environment?' 45 per cent said they had bought products in recycled packaging, 52 per cent had bought products made from recycled materials, 35 per cent had bought environmentally friendly detergents or cleaners, and 33 per cent products in biodegradable packaging. Overall, 42 per cent of people participating in this survey said that they had selected one product over another because of its environmentally friendly packaging, formulation or advertising.

Similar figures on environmentally conscious shopping were also published in Mintel's *The Green Shopper (The Green Consumer Vol. II)* in 1994. According to this survey, 55 per cent of supermarket shoppers are influenced by environmental considerations and 55 per cent are confused by claims on products to be 'environmentally friendly'.

Although these figures appear to provide evidence that many consumer buying decisions are made on environmental grounds, the reported experience of retailers is somewhat different. Back in 1991, Tesco gave evidence to the House of Commons select committee on the environment. Tesco said that its 'dark green' products, designed for the most environmentally conscious shopper, had only a 1 per cent market share, though what were then termed 'environmentally-friendly' (and labelled) products, such as 'green' washing up liquids, had about 7 per cent of the market. Since then, both Tesco and the Co-op have informed us they have stopped carrying many of their own 'green' product ranges because of lack of demand, though recycled paper products have a sizeable and established market.

Further data on the actual extent of 'green' shopping, as opposed to what consumers say they do, is very hard to obtain. We wrote to leading supermarket retailers in an attempt to update the 1991 figures, but none was prepared to reveal them. Mintel, in a 1994 report on household cleaning agents quotes trade evidence that only 2 per cent of products bought in this particular market are 'green' [Mintel, *Monthly Reports*, April 1994]. (Here 'green' is defined as a product designed to be less harmful to the environment, which is either concentrated or packaged in recyclable or refillable containers.)

The survey research

Overall, we had considerable doubts about the evidence for the existence of a vast army of environmentally conscious shoppers. We therefore decided to commission some new market research among shoppers. We felt that the complexity of the issues and the quite complicated decision-making processes involved in consumer purchasing behaviour meant that this subject was best tackled by qualitative research, using discussion groups of ordinary shoppers. The research was conducted in August 1995 and involved six discussion groups. A follow-up discussion group of consumers who appeared to be more environmentally aware was held two months later. The research and its results are discussed in detail in chapter 5.

We also decided that, in order to assess what sorts of claims are in fact being made today, it was necessary to carry out some fairly extensive shopping. We therefore commissioned the Consumers' Association shopping unit, who buy the products tested for *Which?* reports and carry out regular shopping surveys, to go shopping for us. Four researchers each spent four days shopping in mid-July 1995. They covered supermarkets, garden centres, DIY stores, high street shops, health food stores, electrical shops and furniture retailers. Their brief was to identify those products which carried environmental claims and to buy a selection of them or to obtain the product literature where appropriate. Many of the products they bought were shown to people participating in our group discussions. The results are discussed in chapter 3.

We found very few examples of environmental claims in the context of services, other than financial services (which are subject to separate regulation outside the terms of our brief). We have therefore concentrated on products.

Consultation and expert information

Our research among shoppers and the shopping survey did not cover advertised environmental claims in sufficient detail, nor did it tap into the expertise of environmental groups, academics, retailers, trade associations and experts in other countries. We therefore wrote formally to nearly one hundred organisations and individuals (listed in appendix 8), asking for their views on the main issues set out in the research brief. We are very grateful for all the information sent by organisations and individuals. Their opinions, and the valuable information many of them sent, are reflected throughout this report.

In addition to consulting Department of Trade and Industry lawyers, we also commissioned Chris Willet, a lecturer in consumer law at Warwick University, to write a background paper on the legal aspects of environmental claims.

Our brief included a requirement to assess the public expenditure costs of implementing any proposal in our recommendations. We were also asked to identify any significant additional costs or burdens that might fall on private business. In pursuit of this objective, we asked all the individuals and organisations to whom we wrote for their views on this point. We followed up the consultation letter with specific requests for costs information to the CBI

Environment Business Forum and the British Retail Consortium Environment Committee. Unfortunately, none of the organisations and individuals we approached was able to help us, and we have therefore not been able to cost our proposals.

In the next four chapters, we report the findings of our research into the environmental claims now commonly being made (chapter 3) and how those claims stand up (chapter 4), into the views of shoppers (chapter 5), and into the views of manufacturers and retailers (chapter 6).

In the second part of our report, we look at how environmental claims are regulated now and the effectiveness of that regulation (chapters 7 and 8), at various other standards and labelling schemes (chapter 9), and at the situation in some countries outside the UK (chapter 10). Chapter 11 explores the options for regulatory reform.

3. The green claims we found

A mark of modern marketing strategies is the speed with which they change. There had been evidence of the widespread use of environmental marketing claims between 1989 and 1991, and a report prepared for the trading standards division of the London borough of Sutton in 1994 collected claims on one hundred products bought in Sutton shops [Sutton Trading Standards, *Environmental Claims: An evaluation of the use of environmental claims in marketing in the UK*, September 1994]. It was obvious, however, that we needed up-to-date information and from a wider geographical spread.

For advertisements making environmental claims, we contacted all the leading advertising organisations and bodies concerned with monitoring advertising claims. We also collected classified advertisements on an ad hoc basis. For product claims, we carried out the shopping survey to provide an illustration of the types of claims being made on products and to collect any sales literature available. It would be impossible to do an exhaustive survey on product claims, given that the modern supermarket carries over 25,000 different product lines. We are confident, however, that the survey we carried out provides a broad picture of the main environmental claims people are likely to encounter when out shopping.

Advertising claims

Environmental claims made in advertisements, in sale promotions and in direct marketing, except those appearing on radio or television, are all currently regulated by the Advertising Standards Authority (ASA). Those on radio and television are regulated by the Broadcast Advertising Clearance Centre (BACC), the Radio Authority and the Independent Television Commission. (For a discussion of how the regulation of advertising works in relation to environmental claims, please see chapter 7.)

We wrote to all the advertising regulatory and trade organisations asking for their comments on the current situation as regards environmental claims in advertising. They all responded. The general consensus was that advertising is particularly prone to trends and fashions and that the period between 1985 and 1991, in particular, was characterised by an increased use of environmental claims in advertising but that fewer claims of this sort were now being made [Advertising Association, letter to the NCC, 2 August 1995 and BACC, letter to NCC, 27 June 1995].

The decline in the number of environmental claims in advertising may be due to a change in fashion, though a number of possible other causes were suggested. The BACC thought that the 'fairly massive public scepticism about advertisers' motives in making environmental claims' revealed through market research, would have discouraged many advertisers from making such claims, even when they were perfectly legitimate. In the BACC's view, the decline in claims probably had more to do with the difficulties advertisers experienced in making them and the very limited scope of claims, than with action by the regulators. The drop in the number of environmental claims had, however, coincided with the publication of its guidance note on the use of environmental claims in broadcast advertising. The Independent Television Commission (ITC) believes that 'to some extent the guidelines are likely to have deterred advertisers from attempting environmental platforms in cases where the merits of their products would not justify this' [ITC, letter to the NCC, 6 June 1995].

With the growth in the frequency of environmental claims in advertising, the Advertising Standards Authority undertook a two-year monitoring survey which began in 1989. It investigated any environmental claims that it found misleading, and produced a guidance note to advertisers on environmental claims in 1990, which was revised and incorporated into the advertising codes in 1994. However, it has since concluded, 'from the analysis of recent complaints to the ASA, that environmental claims in advertising is no longer quite the problem that it was a few years ago' [ASA, letter to the NCC, 14 July 1995]. Of a total of 9,603 complaints received by the ASA in 1993, 78 related to environmental advertising of which 15 were upheld. In 1994 the proportion was similar - of 9,657 complaints, 89 concerned environmental advertising of which only four were upheld.

Further evidence that, in advertising at least, environmental claims are currently 'less of a problem than they were once' comes from the ASA's recent attempt at a survey. It looked for all advertisements with environmental claims in a comprehensive selection of weekly and monthly magazines and national and regional newspapers during the first two weeks of January 1995. As only one advertisement was found with an environmental claim, the survey was dropped.

Despite all this, environmental claims are still being made in advertisements, if not at the level they were a few years ago. During the course of our review, at least two major national advertising campaigns stressing the environmental credentials of products were under way, one for Elida Gibbs 'Organics' shampoo (subject of a complaint to the ASA by the Soil Association, which was rejected), and one for Reckitt and Colman's 'Down to Earth' range of detergents (subject of two complaints by Lever Bros Ltd, which were upheld by the ASA in March 1994, after which the advertisements were amended). Advertisements by two major environmental groups were also criticised in ASA rulings [*ASA Monthly Report*, October 1995]. We also found some interesting small advertisements in lesser known magazines which are not systematically monitored by the ASA, for products as diverse as 'ecological pond cleaner' and fleecy jackets 'made from 100 per cent recycled polyethylene bottles'. Overall, however, we did not find a vast number of environmental claims being made in advertisements in 1995.

Product claims

The shopping survey we commissioned covered environmental claims made in product literature available in shops, and claims made directly on products, their packaging or on labels attached to the product or the packaging. Four shoppers normally employed by the Consumers' Association to buy products tested for *Which?* magazine each spent four days in mid-July 1995 shopping for the National Consumer Council. One shopper based in Leeds shopped only for groceries, and these were also covered by a Bromley-based shopper who visited major high street retail chains as well. A shopper based in Hertfordshire spent four days looking for environmental claims on gardening and DIY products, and another in Nottingham covered kitchen appliances (white goods) and furniture.

The shoppers found environmental claims in words, and in many different symbols and logos, scattered across a fairly broad spectrum of products and on most types of packaging. Some of the product packaging may also have implied a claim to some sort of environmental superiority, by virtue of being decorated with pictures of dolphins, flowers, waves, waterfalls, birds, green landscapes and rainbows. We have summarised the information about the most common claims on the next two pages. (A complete list of the claims we found is in appendix 1. Symbols and logos relating to environmental claims are reproduced in appendices 2, 3 and 4.)

Written claims

Claim	Type of product
No CFCs	Hairsprays, styling mousses, shaving foam, antiperspirants, bodyspray, fly and wasp killer, insecticides, insect repellent, air fresheners, furniture polish. Also on some refrigerators. Usual wording 'no CFCs', 'CFC free', 'contains no CFC propellant alleged to damage ozone - environmentally responsible'.
Product made from recycled materials	Kitchen towels, toilet rolls, paper tissues, envelopes, greeting cards, rubbish sacks. Wording very variable, included 'made from 100% recycled paper', 'reduces the amount of waste which is landfilled', 'environment friendlier'.
Biodegradable	Shampoo, conditioner, washing powder, hand wash liquid, washing up liquid, fabric conditioner, toilet cleaner, disinfectant, anti-bacterial cleaner, household bleach, some insecticides and fungicides, dishwasher liquid, greetings cards. Wording variable, included 'biodegradable: the cleaning agents are broken down by natural processes', and 'paper used to produce this card and envelope is biodegradable'.
Contains no bleach or optical brighteners	Tissues, baby wipes, toilet paper, washing powder. Wording variable, included 'bleached using low chlorine process, more environmentally responsible than other methods'.

▶ ▶ ▶

Claim	Type of product
Does not contain other specified ingredients	No EDTA, no NTAs, no phosphates, no zeolites, no synthetic colour or perfumes: all on washing powder. No lead: on paint, varnishes. No mercury, no cadmium: on batteries. 'No unnecessary ingredients'.
Product is made from wood or wood pulp from sustainable resources	Some garden and indoor furniture, garden trellis, some paper products.
Does not contain peat, or contains peat from a specified source	Garden composts and mulches.
Packaging is made from recycled materials	Plastic: bleach bottle - wording 'this bottle contains more than 25% recycled plastic'. Cardboard: washing powder box, coffee pack, cereal packet - wording 'this packaging uses 75% recycled board'. Metal: furniture polish, air freshener.
Packaging is recyclable	Washing up liquid bottle - wording variable, included 'label and bottle are made of HDPE, cap of PP. All are 100% recyclable', shampoo and disinfectant bottles, shaving foam can, tuna tin, paint tin etc.
Refill packs	Fabric conditioner, washing powder, baby wipes, washing up liquid, Body Shop products. The wording varies eg. 'this carton is crushable for easy disposal', 'this pack uses approximately 80% less plastic by weight than the parent canister'.

In addition, there was a considerable number of general claims and statements about the environment such as 'ozone friendly', 'environmentally responsible', 'made with concern for the environment', 'made using a process considered to be less harmful to the environment', 'environmentally friendly', 'grown with conservation in mind', 'respecting the environment', 'caring for the environment', 'working for quality and the environment', 'softer on the environment', 'products for a cleaner environment', 'washing ecologically safe', 'no unnecessary ingredients', 'environment friendlier', 'easy on the environment', 'designed with the environment in mind', 'ozone friendlier' and 'environmentally conscious'. (See appendix 1 for the full list of all the environmental claims found by the shoppers.)

Overall, our impression is that the vast majority of environmental claims are on the product labels, the product or its packaging, or they are implied in the design of the product packaging. These may then appear in advertisements, but most written claims are attached to the product itself in some form.

Symbols and logos

Even a cursory inspection of the products bought in the shopping survey revealed that, in addition to written claims about the environment, they carried a wide variety of symbols and logos which made some sort of environmental claim about the product or its packaging, or which could be interpreted to make such a claim. A surprising number of products bore several symbols or logos. Fifty-five of the symbols were removed from the products we found and transferred to sheets of paper to be shown to people during the market research. These sheets are reproduced in appendix 2.

Five different types of symbol or logo appear on products:

- manufacturers' logos, which are really just pictorial marketing claims;

- logos indicating that the product had been endorsed in some way by a non-official body such as a charity or environmental group;

- approval marks with some sort of national official or government endorsed status;

- approval marks with an international status;

- markings on packaging which either specify the materials used or how to dispose of the packaging.

In fact most of the logos and symbols we found were either manufacturers' marketing claims or packaging symbols. There are comparatively few bodies which provide approval marks or product endorsements. (Further details of some of the best known schemes are in chapter 9.) The most important point about all these different logos and symbols is that, unless the consumer is familiar with them, the different types are indistinguishable. An approval mark or product endorsement logo can look exactly like a marketing claim or a packaging symbol.

The logos and symbols used in marketing claims cover every environmental aspect of the product. One of the most common symbols is a picture of the globe, but 'caring' hands and representation of water, mountains, clouds, rainbows and the sky are also frequently used. They tend to be printed in green or blue ink. A common image in claims about the absence of chlorofluoro carbons was a white arc. We have come to the conclusion that this is supposed to represent the ozone layer. Sometimes the globe was altered into a heart shape, presumably to indicate caring. Rabbits, dolphins, trees, flowers, birds and a bee also featured in some of these marketing symbols.

In addition to manufacturers' symbols and approval marks, many of the products in our shopping survey carried symbols which, to those in the know, describe the composition of the packaging material used and how to dispose of it or, like the green dot symbol (see appendix 2, symbol number 30), indicate only that the manufacturer of the product has paid a fee for the packaging to enter either the German or French packaging reclamation systems (though not that it necessarily will be recycled). It is arguable that the markings are not really environmental claims since they are describing only the composition of the packaging or, in the case of the green dot, that a fee has been paid.

The people who carried out our shopping survey were asked not to buy products that carried only markings about the composition of the packaging material. However, the markings are also sometimes used in conjunction with written claims or exhortations, such as 'please recycle' or 'recyclable where facilities exist'. Their function may be to draw attention or to emphasise the wording, or to add an impression of official status to the words used, so in this context they are used as part of an environmental claim. (For a discussion of some of these markings, see chapter 4.)

The appearance of *der grüne Punkt* (the green dot) on UK packaging adds another logo to the many already being used and another possible area for confusion. Again, it is not strictly an environmental claim, or certainly not in the UK, though it could be taken for one. The green dot symbol was originally developed in Germany in response to the German packaging ordinance. Under this, firms using packaging materials have to take used packaging back and ensure it will be recycled. Consumer packaging is all collected and recycled by one German company, DSD. The green dot is proof that the firm has registered their packaging with DSD and paid a fee, based on the quantity and type of material. DSD then takes over responsibility for collecting the used packaging from households and recycling it [see *Waste 92: a study on the testing of perceptibility, readability and understanding of markings of products at consumer level*, Denmark for the European Union, 1994]. The green dot is also an indication for consumers that packaging thus marked can be put in the special containers whose contents are supposed to be recycled. Although the scheme is voluntary, it has become virtually obligatory because German retailers will not accept packaged goods that are not marked.

The green dot is also used on packaging in France but unfortunately it means something slightly different. Again it is neither obligatory nor official but is becoming so, as retailers have begun to insist on it [see Michel Barnier, *'Les logos écologiques' des produits et de leurs emballages*, Environment Ministry, Paris, January 1995]. In France, the green dot means that the packaging manufacturer has paid the contribution required under the French packaging law which goes towards creating a national system for 'valorising' waste packaging. Valorising means extracting the worth of the material; it can include composting, incineration or even landfill under certain conditions, and may include recycling when a national system for collecting materials for recycling has been established.

British-based manufacturers and retailers with markets in France and Germany must comply with the local laws, and so have joined the French and German schemes to recycle, or valorise, their packaging waste. For a company like Marks and Spencer, the result is that much of their packaging - whether or not it ultimately ends up in France and Germany - now carries the green dot, or one of the logos of the various other French and German schemes for dealing with transit packaging. Although these symbols actually do not mean anything in the UK context, some people in our market research groups interpreted them to be an environmental claim.

Several other studies have commented on the vast number of environmental symbols and logos. The French study (mentioned above) discussed forty-four different *logos écologiques*. While the author was pleased to find that concern about the environment was now so central to marketing, he was worried that the message was becoming confused by the sheer number of logos and the many trade marks, trade names and less explicit signs which seek to give a product 'green' credentials. The Sutton study, too, commented on 'the proliferation of "green" symbols'. The study by Denmark for the EU also comments on the 'proliferation of symbols on packaging' as part of 'efforts to convince consumers how environmentally friendly it is'. It found that manufacturers in general were confused about which sign to use, the rules on which they are based, and whether there is a need for registration in order to use a sign or for official sanction.

The authors comment: 'the fact is, however, that a variety of signs can be seen on packaging. No system can be observed in the use of signs even within the same firm ... A number of surveys show that most consumers are not able to tell the proper meaning of even the most commonly used signs.'

4. An assessment of the claims we found

The environmental claims made on or about products and/or their packaging can be categorised in a number of different ways. From the consumer point of view, one useful way is to sort claims into those where the manufacturer or person making the claim is responsible for any environmental benefits, and those where the consumer or someone else bears at least part of the burden. So for instance, claims about ingredients or the use of recycled components or packaging place the burden squarely on the manufacturer, while those about the recyclability of the product or its packaging, or about refill packs, leave the harvesting of any environmental gain to the consumer.

It is our impression that the trend in environmental claims is towards greater use of the second type of claim, where the consumer has to do something in order to activate the environmental benefits. This may be something to do with the current trend towards using refill packs for a wider variety of products than in the recent past. This appears to satisfy a dual need - for manufacturers of bulky products to reduce the size on environmental and cost grounds, and for consumers, critical of excess packaging, to see an immediate economic benefit in using refills as well as greater convenience.

Another way of categorising claims is to take a more legalistic approach, and divide them into those that are straightforward, those that are hard to verify and therefore to prove or disprove, and those that are, or could be, misleading.

How honest and truthful?

Unverifiable claims must be taken on trust. This is true not just for consumers, for whom this frequently applies, but also for people with a professional interest in product claims, such as trading standards officers. Unverifiable claims include those where no amount of product testing will shed any light on the truthfulness of the claims. This particularly applies to claims about the *sources* of products, such as timber from managed or sustainable forests, peat that does not come from a site of special scientific interest, or tuna that is caught using a line rather than a net. It also applies to some claims about the *content*, such as 'contains X per cent of recycled fibre', when applied to paper or textiles. Similarly, claims about the recycled content of metal and glass containers cannot be verified through testing. It is also not possible to test plastics to verify the proportion of recycled materials (see Sutton Trading Standards, *Environmental Claims: An evaluation of the use of environmental claims in marketing in the UK*, already mentioned in chapter 3, which tried to do this for plastic sacks).

Other claims may be narrowly true, and verifiable, but actually meaningless in a wider context. Examples include negative ingredient listing, where no products, or only a tiny minority of products in this class, contain this ingredient, so the benefit claimed is specious.

We found several examples of this. Some washing powders claim not to contain 'NTAs or EDTAs' but NTAs have been banned from washing powders in the USA and neither ingredient has been used much at all in Europe [Soap and Detergent Industry Association]. Some washing liquids claim not to contain phosphates, but again these are not normally used in washing liquids. Many toiletries, as well as most aerosols, claim not to contain CFCs (chlorofluoro carbons). However, the only products currently on the market which contain CFCs are the inhalers used by asthmatics and even these may be on the way out ['Dispelling the green fears', *Times*, 12 September 1995]. Most aerosols have been CFC-free since 1989 [British Aerosol Manufacturers' Association].

To claim 'green credentials' as a result of not using a product that has been banned is arguably misleading. Lead has not been added to household paints since the 1970s, but we found several examples (see appendix 1) of household paints and varnishes which carried the product claim that no lead had been added.

Other misleading claims include those which present a feature as a positive environmental benefit when it is not, or not necessarily. For example, 'biodegradable' is generally viewed as a positive description when it is applied to a product. But it is not an appropriate claim for paper in the UK, given that most waste paper is disposed of in landfill sites and current archaeological evidence is that it rots very slowly. Similarly, degradable plastic bags also rot very slowly, and leave a residue, so may be best incinerated where there are the facilities. The management of landfill sites is, in any case, designed to inhibit the biodegradation of the contents.

Some claims are drawn so narrowly that, although they are truthful in what they say, they mask a wider falsehood and are therefore potentially misleading. For example, an aerosol with the claim that 'this product contains no propellant alleged to damage the ozone layer' might contain other ingredients which could damage the ozone layer or contribute to other environmental problems. Similarly, the claim that 'for each tree felled three more are planted' may be true but it ignores the potential negative environmental impact of this type of intensive monocultural forestry.

Also potentially misleading are environmental claims which are truthful but which apply to all products in the class, whether they make the claim or not. 'CFC free' falls into this category, as do 'biodegradable' when it is applied to the surface active agents (explained later in this section) used in washing powders, 'recyclable' (which is theoretically almost always true, but may well not happen in practice), and claims that the product contains recycled material when some industries, such as steel, aluminum and the manufacture of certain types of board, have used scraps as a proportion of raw material for years.

Other claims lack accepted definitions, and so could mean virtually anything. 'Recycled' is a particularly troublesome claim in this regard. What proportion of the product has to be recycled for such a claim to be truthful? Does it matter how much of the product is made from waste recycled after consumers have used it, or is it acceptable to make this claim when the only recycling done is of scraps reclaimed during the manufacturing process? The Sutton Trading Standards report considered this claim in relation to plastic rubbish sacks. Since very little plastic rubbish is recycled in the UK (see below for more information on this), it concluded that most of the recycled plastic used in rubbish sacks does not come from a post-consumer source. Moreover, the term 'recycled' was used on products containing 30 per cent, 50 per cent or 60 per cent recycled material, judging by the product claims.

The most common environmental claims of all, to judge from our survey, do not fall into any of the above categories. These are the vague and woolly claims which try to convey a positive impression about concern for the environment, but which may in fact be completely deceptive. Claims such as 'softer on the environment', 'caring for the environment', 'made with conservation in mind', 'respects the environment' and 'environmentally friendly' may be true, and may even be capable of substantiation. But, equally, they may be unreliable or false and so misleading to anyone relying on them.

Although the claims we found were scattered across a wide range of goods, the products which attracted the most claims were detergents, all aerosols, all types of packaging and, generally associated with packaging materials, recycling claims. In order to provide some detailed advice to the Department of the Environment, we examined the veracity and usefulness to consumers of claims about packaging, recycling, detergents and aerosols.

Packaging

Households in this country produce around 20 million tonnes of waste a year. Five million tonnes of this is taken to municipal dumps by householders. Most of the rest is collected by the dustmen. About a quarter of a typical dustbin's contents consists of used packaging [Industry Council for Packaging and the Environment, *Briefing on Recycling*, November 1993]. Most household waste ends up as landfill where it forms about 10 per cent of the 150 million tonnes of waste buried in the UK every year.

The packaging industry is under concerted government and European Union pressure to reduce the amount of packaging that goes into landfill. The UK government has tackled the issue from three angles. From 1996 there will be a tax on landfill charges, to provide a financial incentive to look for alternative means of waste disposal or recycling. Secondly, in 1993, the government challenged the packaging industry to come up with a plan, financed by some sort of levy on producers and/or heavy commercial users of packaging, for recovering between 50 per cent and 75 per cent of packaging waste by 2000. Although the industry has reached agreement on a scheme to achieve a target of 58 per cent of used packaging to be recovered by 2000, they have yet to work out how it will be funded. Finally, in the government's 'waste strategy for England and Wales' introduced in January 1995, there is a new target for recycling 50 per cent of the component of household waste that is capable of being recycled by 2000. Much of this will be waste packaging.

In addition, the UK has enacted the European Union directive on packaging and packaging waste [Directive 94/62, European Commission]. Under this measure, each state is required to set up systems to recover between 50 per cent and 65 per cent of packaging waste, to recycle between 25 per cent and 45 per cent of it, and to ensure that a minimum recycling level of 15 per cent of waste is achieved for each individual material. By 1998 packaging will only be allowed into the market if it conforms to certain requirements. These include the minimisation of weight and volume, its suitability for re-use, and the ability to recycle its component materials or to use them for energy recovery or for composting.

With the exception of the landfill tax, all these measures are very likely to generate additional environmental claims and symbols on packaging in the next few years. Indeed the EU directive establishes a marking system to help with the recovery of used packaging which, under current proposals, will introduce some new symbols on packaging. It is worth considering, however, whether packaging symbols are useful to the consumer at all, and whether they will in fact help in the pre-sorting of rubbish that will be necessary if the recycling targets for domestic rubbish are to be achieved.

Packaging materials are made from glass, aluminium, steel, paper or plastics, or a combination of these. Glass forms 6 per cent to 8 per cent of household waste: it is heavy, not easily burnt, and does not biodegrade. But it is easily recognised and sorted from other packaging, and about one in three glass bottles is now recycled, mainly through bottle banks ['Market forces harnessed in drive to recycle waste', *Guardian*, 15 July 1995]. Since it is easy to recognise, there is no obvious need to mark glass containers in any way. However, the tidyman and bottlebank symbol (see appendix 3, packaging symbol number 1) is widely used on glass bottles to remind consumers to dispose of the bottle in a bottlebank. Research commissioned by INCPEN found this was one symbol that was widely recognised and understood by consumers [Jayne Windus Associates for INCPEN, *Report on Anti Littering Messages*, 1995].

Aluminium, mainly cans, forms about 1 per cent of household waste. About 80 per cent of soft drinks and 66 per cent of beers are packaged in aluminium cans [Mintel, *Recycling*, October 1994]. About a quarter of aluminium cans are recycled, mainly through Save-A-Can schemes run by charities and local authorities. Most of these schemes do not distinguish between cans made of aluminium and of steel.

Steel forms 6 per cent of household waste and is again widely recycled. Some municipal waste sites have giant magnets which are used to extract ferrous metals. Other can-collection schemes also use magnets to sort the cans. Twenty-five per cent of every new steel can is made from recycled steel. It is not really necessary for consumers to sort cans according to their metal content and so not strictly necessary to label cans with their metal content. However, most cans do now carry symbols to indicate metal content. (For the two symbols most widely used on cans, see appendix 3, packaging symbol numbers 3 and 4.)

Paper packaging forms about 6 per cent of household waste, though paper from other sources like newspapers and magazines take up a much higher proportion. Paper is readily identified, and most collectors sort it anyway, in order to extract certain treated papers and colours. It does not need to be labelled.

Plastics form a tiny proportion of household packaging waste as they are so light and thin but, like glass, they do not rot, although they do burn at high temperatures. They pose an additional problem for recycling in that there are at least six types of plastic used in packaging, and they need to be separated and sorted before they can be re-used or recycled. Plastics are sometimes classified by their end use: rigid plastics, such as yogurt pots and bottles are relatively easy to collect; plastic films and wrappers, which form up to 4 per cent of household waste, are very difficult to recycle, as the process of cleaning, sorting and de-inking is complicated, messy and expensive.

There are very few schemes for collecting plastic waste from consumers for recycling. If, under the impetus of the EU directive, these schemes take off, consumers may well be asked to pre-sort rigid plastics by type of plastic or to separate all rigid plastics from their waste for sorting by collectors. In this case, the labelling of plastics by type could be important. Many manufacturers of rigid plastic containers currently follow the American SPI labelling scheme (see appendix 3, packaging symbol number 2). Generally, these symbols are not prominent but are to be found on the bottom of bottles or in the least noticed part of the product label. There has been no attempt to tell consumers what they mean, and the consumers in our discussion groups did not understand them. Without an effective public information campaign, it would be very difficult to use these as a basis for a massive recycling effort by consumers. It looks as if sorting of plastics into the different types of plastic materials will have to be done by collectors.

In short, with the possible exception of plastics, there is no great need to mark packaging materials in order to promote the recovery of used packaging. Evidence from our market research shows that consumers do not understand, and seldom take much notice of, the marks currently in use. The main types of packaging material are in any case readily distinguishable, without the need for marking.

Meeting the packaging recovery targets will require a sustained public information campaign to encourage people to sort their household rubbish and different collection systems for refuse.

Recycling

For many consumers, concern for the environment is virtually synonymous with efforts to recycle waste. People in our discussion groups who wished to establish their environmental credentials were most likely to mention their efforts to recycle their own rubbish and to buy recycled products. This is hardly surprising: the environmental movement in the UK first achieved national notice when Friends of the Earth dumped a load of no-deposit bottles at the doors of Schweppes in protest at the ending of its national collection and refill system for bottled soft drinks. Although that was twenty years ago, recycling is still perceived as one of the foremost environmental issues (for evidence, see NOP, *Public Attitudes to the Environment*, July-August 1993, discussed in chapter 2). This partly explains why there are so many environmental claims about recyclability and recycling.

Environmentalists, on the other hand, have moved on from focusing concern on recycling. For example, Friends of the Earth no longer has a recycling officer. Greater emphasis is now given to minimising the amount of materials and energy used in the manufacture of products, to re-using products and then only to recycling the components when the previous processes have been exhausted. That the overall goal should be to minimise the use of resources in the first place is perhaps the one area where leading environmental groups and the packaging industry are in total agreement [INCPEN see *Briefing on Recycling*, November 1993].

The problem with recycling is that it has its own environmental costs, particularly the consumption of energy required to collect, sort and reprocess waste, but also the release of toxic residues. For example, kitchen appliances (white goods) are generally shredded for their metal content. But old appliances may have capacitors and transformers which contain toxic PCBs (polychlorinated biphenyl), old refrigerators contain CFCs (chlorofluoro carbons), and they may also contain heavy metals such as cadmium, which is used as a colouring medium and stabiliser in plastics. Shredder waste from vehicles may be heavily polluted with oils, heavy metals and hydrocarbons. All this waste is buried in landfill sites [Tim Cooper, *Beyond Recycling*, New Economics Foundation, November 1994].

The Mobius muddle

The Mobius Loop was the only symbol relating to packaging which people who took part in our market research recognised. They interpreted it, correctly, to mean *either* that the product or its packaging were recyclable *or* that some proportion or all of it had been recycled. Clearly, these two meanings are different so what is the symbol supposed to mean, and where does it come from?

Mobius Loop (ISO)

There are two versions of the Mobius Loop. The symbol with curved arrows has been registered with the International Standards Organisation (ISO), while the triangle which incorporates the arrows is registered by the German standards organisation, DIN. The ISO version originated in the USA, and the rights to use it in Europe were once owned by Continental Can, the US company. In Europe the company took action in the Benelux courts to enforce its copyright. As a result, the symbol was dropped in those countries, though it has continued to be used widely, particularly on cardboard and

Mobius Loop (DIN)

paper, elsewhere in Europe. In some countries, such as Finland, it is only ever used on paper and cardboard. However, the rights to use the symbol in Europe now belongs to a trade association, the European Portable Battery Manufacturers' Association. It has been trying to promote a marking scheme for small batteries, to show they can be recycled. It is possible they may one day act to restrict use of the symbol by anyone else.

In Germany, the DIN version of the Mobius Loop is used with a number (from 01 to 07) to indicate the type of plastic used in packaging in order to help consumers to sort out their rubbish. This system is similar to the American SPI system for marking plastics (see appendix 3) which is used in the UK and many other countries. At present, the ISO is pressing ahead with plans to use the Mobius loop, but with several different meanings. The European Portable Battery Manufacturers' Association has had its use of the symbol on batteries, to denote recyclability, recognised in a draft standard produced by the ISO committee (TC 145) on graphic symbols. Meanwhile, the ISO working group on environmental claims (TC 207) has proposed that the symbol be used on both packaging and products to mean either 'recyclable' or 'contains recycled material' though it will always be accompanied by an explanatory text. The ISO standard will be voluntary.

Unfortunately, these proposals are at variance with the current EU proposals for the marking of packaging under the Packaging Waste Directive, which may eventually be mandatory for EU members. The EU proposals are still under discussion and are subject to change. One proposal is that recoverable (or recyclable) packaging will carry a broken circular arrow (see appendix 3). The EU has also proposed two new symbols, one for re-usable packaging, and the other, which will be optional, to show that a certain proportion of the packaging is made from recycled materials. The EU, because of the language problem, does not favour the use of text.

Some raw materials have always been reclaimed from scrap because of their high intrinsic value. Claims that kitchen appliances and cars are somehow more recyclable nowadays are a myth, because their high metal content has always been valued by scrap merchants. In fact, as the metal content is reduced and the proportion made of plastics rises, these products are gradually becoming less valuable as scrap. The average percentage of materials recycled from the two million vehicles scrapped annually in Britain is currently 77 per cent [Tim Cooper, see above] but most of the rest (thermosetting plastics, rubber foam, textiles and fluids) cannot be recycled.

There are, however, some major industry initiatives under way to re-use car parts. BMW, prompted by the proposed 'take back' legislation in Germany that will require manufacturers to take responsibility for their products once discarded, has established a plant in Sussex where its cars are dismantled and some parts reclaimed. About three-quarters of all white goods are shredded for their metal content, but most brown goods (TVs, radios, stereo equipment, electric fires and so on) end up as landfill. Some major electronic companies do now take back used equipment.

Paper is another product which has been routinely recycled for many years. Up to one third of household waste is paper, and recycled paper is used in around 60 per cent of UK production of paper and board [Mintel, *Recycling*, October 1994]. However, these two facts are scarcely connected, since the source of most paper that is recycled is the paper industry itself. Paper mills deal with two types of waste paper - either undifferentiated waste, where all types of paper are mushed together and turned into products such as cardboard transit packaging, or high-grade waste. The latter is obtained from the following sources, in order of preference: mill off cuts; converters' off cuts (for example, paper carton manufacturers' waste); white paper waste from big users such as offices; and lastly households, mostly in the form of newspapers which are put to one side and collected by local groups or taken to paper banks. Very little paper is reclaimed from dustbins as it is too contaminated with food or coated with other materials like plastics and coloured inks.

Environmental claims about recycled paper seldom take account of the fact that most recycling takes place before the 'recycled' paper ever reaches the consumer. The evidence from our discussion groups is that most people seem to think that recycling refers to the collection and re-use of paper after it has been used by consumers. Indeed, some people in our groups expressed the fear - or belief - that recycled toilet tissue has passed through the sewage system at least once before. However, when the distinction between pre- and post-consumer recycling was pointed out to people, they were not concerned about where in the product chain the recycling had occurred. As far as they were concerned it all helped to save scant resources.

In general, glass recycling schemes have been a success - around 30 per cent of UK glass packaging was recycled in 1994, though this compares with up to 80 per cent in Germany and Denmark. The recycling rates for metals are also good. Around 25 per cent of aluminium cans and 12 per cent of steel cans are recycled now, and this is set to rise as more local authorities introduce magnetic extraction for steel. The recent rise in demand for used newspapers, prompted by the opening of a new mill at Aylesford in Kent, means that it is once again profitable to recycle newspapers.

The real problem area is still plastics. The main types of plastic are incompatible, so they have to be sorted into categories. This is done, where it is done, mainly by hand and so is expensive. Plastics are frequently used in contact with food, as a result of which they are potentially contaminated and cannot be recycled for food use. At present, for these reasons, about 90 per cent of the plastic recycled is made from scrap reclaimed during the manufacturing process. Most of the rest is polyethylene film, which is used to wrap pallets when goods are being transported, and is recycled into plastic sheeting and refuse sacks. Some polypropylene is also recycled from bottle crates, transit packaging and vehicle batteries into drainage pipes and injection mouldings [Mintel, *Recycling*, October 1994]. The polyester fibre in polyethylene terephthalate bottles can also be reclaimed for the textile industry. We found fleecy jackets of the type worn by walkers made from fibres reclaimed from bottles. Currently, prices for polyester are high and can make recycling plastic bottles profitable, but this is not always so ['Market forces harnessed in drive to recycle waste', *Guardian*, 15 July 1995].

The future of plastics recycling is uncertain, given the difficulties and high cost. Two possible avenues may help the plastics industry meet the UK government and European Union targets on recycling. One is the development of a pilot plant by BP and a group of companies at Grangemouth. This plant uses fairly well-established technology to convert mixed plastics back into high quality petrochemicals feedstock which can then be used to make the basic constituents of plastic again [Environmental Data Services *ENDS Report*, January 1994]. The main problem with this approach is the high economic and environmental costs of collecting, transporting and 'cracking' the used plastics.

The other approach, which is being adopted in France and is fairly common in Germany, is to incinerate plastic rubbish. Plastics burn at a high temperature and so generate useful amounts of energy while they do not take up much space. If the energy generated can be re-used (or valorised), this can make environmental sense, although it would require substantial investment in new municipal incinerators if it were to be applied on a wide scale.

Overall, the consumers in our groups were interested in recycling claims and most claimed to buy, or to have bought, recycled paper products and to have recycled glass and sometimes newspapers. They expected recycling claims to refer to 100 per cent of the content unless told otherwise, though they accepted that even a recycled content as low as 30 per cent was evidence of some effort on the part of manufacturers. When pressed, although they generally assumed that recycling claims referred to recycling after the consumer had used the product, no one in either the main groups or the follow-up group objected to recycling claims being made about materials reclaimed during the manufacturing process. When pressed, they tended to agree that claims that products were 'recyclable' were superfluous.

Detergents

Detergents for washing clothes and dishes carry many competing environmental claims. These vary from the WWF (World Wildlife Fund) panda logo, found on Ariel Ultra washing powder packs, to long and quite complicated environmental panels on the side of boxes (Persil), to products entirely centred on environmental claims, such as the Ecover range and Sainsbury's Greencare. In our consumer research, people talked at length about detergents, why they chose the brands they used, and the environmental issues they perceived to be connected with them. For people in our follow-up group, use of 'green' detergents and cleaning products was almost a credential for judging environmental awareness. It is interesting to speculate why environmental claims have become so important to marketing this range of products.

The UK detergent market is dominated by two fiercely competitive marketing-driven companies, Lever and Procter & Gamble. Both use intensive advertising to try and capture greater market share. In a market worth around £750 million in 1993, these two companies spent over £88 million on advertising washing powders alone. Lever's Persil and Procter & Gamble's Ariel are the most popular brands, followed by Daz and Bold (both Procter & Gamble) [see 'Coming Out in the Wash', *Marketing Week*, 18 November 1994, p. 36]. The hold of these two companies over the market has been challenged only by supermarkets' own brands. Most of the advertising (and these two companies are consistently the UK's top two spenders on advertising) has changed little in emphasis over many years. For example, the recent Daz campaign incorporating the slogan 'Would your whites pass the Daz doorstep challenge?' complete with pretty suburban housewife and frenetic doorstep promotion man, could have been lifted from campaigns thirty years ago.

In this context, the launch of 'green' detergents in the late 1980s, with strong environmental messages, was a fresh marketing challenge in a tired market and may help to explain the original appeal of such products and the response in kind by the leading manufacturers. All the washing powder manufacturers now make environmental claims, though not on every brand. Environmental claims on detergents fall into a number of different categories. Negative ingredients are commonly listed, so are claims about biodegradability. Other claims relate to saving the quantities used (particularly the concentrated powders), to their use at low temperatures (with consequent energy savings), and claims about the recyclability or re-use of the packaging with the aid of refill packs.

The claims about ingredients are technical and quite complex. Generally, washing powders and liquids have complicated formulations and the ingredients are inter-related. So if one ingredient is reduced or removed, it is quite probable that another will have to be increased. The main environmental claims relating to washing powders have been tested by the trading standards department of the Central Regional Council in Scotland [Maggie Gibbons-Loveday, *Washing Powders - Clean and Green?* Institute of Trading Standards Administration, 1995]. They found that many washing powders claimed to be biodegradable. However, on closer examination, these claims related to their surface active agents (surfactant). Most powders contain surfactants, which are the basic cleaning ingredients. These can be of many kinds but only anionic and non-ionic surfactants are required by EU regulation to be biodegradable. In fact, the UK detergents industry voluntarily introduced biodegradable surfactant in the 1960s when there was a problem with foam in the rivers. The UK standards on biodegradability exceed the levels set by the EU, so there is no need to label the products as biodegradable.

Many of the environmental claims about detergents are about other product ingredients called 'builders'. Builders allow the other ingredients to function efficiently by softening the water and altering its acidity balance. They include phosphates, carbonates, silicates, citrates, zeolites (aluminosilicates) and polycarboxylic acid (PCA). The use of phosphates in detergents has been criticised as contributing to eutrophication - the over-fertilisation of ponds and slow moving waters which causes algae to multiply and other forms of life to die. Detergents have been estimated (in a study by Imperial College) to contribute 19 per cent of the phosphates present in UK surface waters, less than human sewage (24 per cent) and farm livestock (29 per cent), but still a significant proportion.

Phosphate-free detergents generally replace phosphates with builders called zeolites, which are not a plant nutrient and so cannot cause eutrophication. Unfortunately, they are ineffective on their own and must be used with a co-builder, usually sodium carbonate and polycarboxylic acid (PCA). These are not considered to be completely harmless - sodium carbonate can cause the alkalinity of water to rise, and PCAs do not biodegrade readily. One study by environmental consultants, commissioned by phosphate producer Albright and Wilson, concluded that there was no real difference between the environmental impacts of the two competing detergent builder systems [*ENDS Report*, November 1994]. Whether or not this is correct, there seems very little basis for the competing environmental claims currently made about the builders in detergents. A longer-term solution may arise in that the EU directive on urban waste water treatment sets standards for the removal of nutrients from sewage where the discharges are to be made into water where eutrophication might occur. Removal of phosphates in sewage works should solve this problem, in which case the environmental claims would be less relevant.

Many washing powders claim not to contain chlorine bleaches. This is usually true, very few do. The bleach most commonly used, sodium perborate, is oxygen-based. Its efficiency increases with the temperature of the wash, so an additive, tetra acetyl ethylene diamine (TAED), is normally added to activate the bleach at low temperatures. The use of sodium perborate in detergents contributed 4,000 tonnes of boron, a water-soluble nutrient, to the environment in 1992 compared with 1,500 tonnes from industrial sources [DoE sources, quoted by Maggie Gibbons-Loveday, see above]. Too much boron applied to crops causes them to die. There are varying standards for acceptable levels of boron in water, though none is currently being breached.

The Central Regional Council study tested 47 washing powders (excluding 'colour care' powders) for their phosphorous and boron content and their powers of stain removal. It found that some of the phosphate-free powders contained small amounts of phosphonates, a form of phosphorous. Although, overall, these powders still contained less phosphorous than those that used phosphates as builders, the author commented that 'it is perhaps misleading to highlight the fact that these powders do not contain phosphates, if they do contain phosphonates'. The results of the wash tests showed that the presence of bleaching agents was crucial to stain removal, and the addition of enzymes (the 'bio' powders) helped further on some stains. It did not make a significant difference whether phosphates were used as builders or not: both types of powder gave results ranging from very good to very poor on all the stains.

As regards environmental claims in general, it seems that some washing powders are marketed on the basis of their environmental credentials, but these can be no better or worse for the environment than other powders marketed by the same manufacturer. This is, perhaps, fairly typical of a market dominated by two manufacturers of much the same product. Every marketing angle must be explored, even when the claims on one product are inconsistent with those on another brand owned by the same company. On specific claims, none of the 47 powders tested by Central Regional Council contained chlorine bleaches, NTA or EDTA, so the claimed absence of these ingredients could be misleading. Furthermore, the biodegradable claim is clearly unnecessary, but if it is to be made, it must be clear that it applies only to the surfactant and not to all the other ingredients. The report concludes: 'if the amount of phosphates and bleaching agent are an indication of green credentials, it does not appear that washing powders can be clean and green'.

The advice from *Which*? for the environmentally conscious launderer is to use a cooler wash temperature, to buy a concentrated detergent which uses fewer chemicals, less packaging and is cheaper to transport, to use refill packs, and not to use too much powder ['Detergents', *Which*?, July 1994]. The Central Regional Council study also suggests using bleach-free powders (the colour care ranges are bleach-free) for laundry which is not badly stained, the removal of stubborn stains by hand, and a reduction in the use of the washing machine.

Aerosols

Aerosols containing a wide range of products from air fresheners to shaving foam tend to carry environmental claims. Sometimes they are confined to stating that the product is 'CFC-free' which has been true for most of them since 1989. Others make more expansive claims such as 'caring for the environment' while some contain more specific information about the propellants used. Since CFCs were phased out, they have been replaced by three alternatives: 'trigger' or 'pump and spray' packs which do not use a propellant at all; butane; or compressed air.

Butane, the most popular replacement for CFCs, has been criticised on environmental grounds, as it is a volatile organic compound (VOC). VOCs can contribute to atmospheric pollution as they collect in the lower atmosphere and react with sunlight to form photo-chemical smog and low-level ozone. Ozone at low level is a pollutant that can trigger asthma and other respiratory diseases. Butane also carries other disadvantages in that it is highly inflammable and is used in solvent abuse ['Dispelling the green fears', *Times*, 12 September 1995, B2 section]. Given these disadvantages, and the development of new aerosol technology by the US company SC Johnson, it is questionable whether any aerosol which uses butane as a propellant could justify a positive environmental claim.

SC Johnson Wax produces the Pledge and Sparkle range of furniture polish, which have a 37 per cent share of the UK market for furniture polish. Since late 1994 the company has replaced butane as a propellant with compressed air. In order to do this, it had to change the formulation of its product and use a stronger can. Using compressed air instead of butane has reduced the product's VOC content from 30 per cent to 20 per cent, a level similar to or less than in trigger sprays [*ENDS Report*, May 1994]. The company makes much of its innovation in its on-pack claims.

In future, it seems likely that the use of butane as a propellant in aerosols will become less common, as consumers switch to trigger sprays and other manufacturers adopt the compressed air technology. Aerosols in general were perceived by consumers in our groups to pose several environmental problems. While most knew that they no longer contained CFCs, the problems associated with using them (wasteful, and unpleasant to inhale when spraying) and with disposal (can must not be punctured or incinerated) led most to conclude that they were best avoided, where possible.

5.   The consumer view: our research with shoppers

The results of our shopping survey and our consultation with the advertising organisations showed that environmental claims are scattered across a fairly wide range of products, and that they do still crop up in advertising, though perhaps less so than in the recent past (chapter 3). Our assessment of the claims we found showed that many are confusing, woolly, and actually or potentially misleading to consumers (chapter 4). However, in order to respond to the first aim of this review, which was to establish the *extent* to which consumers are being affected by false or misleading claims, we needed to find out whether people were aware of claims, whether they attached much credence to them, whether the claims influenced their choice of product when deciding what to buy, and whether they were confused or misled by them.

The fairly complex decision-making processes involved in choosing goods when out shopping are an endless source of interest to anyone marketing products or services, to marketing academics, and to consumer bodies like the National Consumer Council [see our book *Your Food: Whose Choice?* published by HMSO, 1992]. Because of the complexity of the issues involved, we decided at an early stage of this project to concentrate on qualitative research among small groups of consumers. In designing the research, the key questions we set out to answer were:

(a)   are consumers aware of environmental claims on products and in advertisements?

(b)   do they look for them when out shopping?

(c)   do they want environmental claims on products?

(d)   do they understand the wording of claims or are they misled by them?

(e)   what would make them more confident about environmental claims?

Characteristics of the people who took part in the research

Six group discussions, each with eight people, were held in August 1995, three in Sheffield and three in Bracknell. Those participating were carefully selected to encompass a good spread of ages and all social groups, and to exclude members of consumer and environmental organisations, or anyone who might be informed above the average level on this subject. The participants were regular shoppers who listed 'concern about the environment' as one among many other considerations they bore in mind when they went shopping. In each group, no more than three participants did most of their shopping at any one particular supermarket. None had ever taken part in such a group before: four of the groups were of women and two of men. We refer to all these groups as 'ordinary shoppers'. The discussions were led by Heather Wild, an independent qualitative researcher with considerable experience in this type of research.

As might be expected from their low incidence in the population, very few avowedly 'green' consumers were present in the original groups. So we decided to follow up with a group of nine women shoppers who were more environmentally aware. This group met in October 1995. Using information based on the experience of the ordinary shoppers, this group was recruited on the basis that they agreed that 'whether the product is environmentally friendly' was a factor they thought about when choosing what to buy, and that it influenced them when out shopping. They were also asked an unprompted question about which environmentally friendly products they made a point of buying. Those who mentioned at least six products, one of which was a detergent or household cleaner, were invited to participate in the group discussion. In order to distinguish them from the other groups, this group was called the 'light greens'.

The views of the 'ordinary' shoppers

During the discussions, people in the first six groups learnt a great deal about environmental claims from the packs and examples shown to them (although initially they did not know this was the purpose of the discussion). Near the beginning, they were asked whether they had noticed *any* marketing claims on products. A few mentioned seeing environmental claims. Someone in all the groups recalled seeing 'recycled' on products, and almost all had noticed 'biodegradable', 'ozone-friendly' and 'CFC free'. People in four out of the six groups had seen claims about rain forests, and sustained and renewable resources, and half the groups came up with 'organic', 'recyclable' and 'environmentally friendly' while one or two mentioned claims about no bleach, saving energy or saving water.

Overall, however, the environment was not a big consideration when they went shopping. If they bought 'green' products at all, they were the ones that were easy to find, such as unleaded petrol and recycled paper products. But it was clear that not much effort was put into seeking out green varieties of products, a view summed up by a woman in Sheffield: 'I don't mooch, ferreting for environmentally friendly ones. If they really stand out then I'll go for it and think "I've done my bit".' If they bought products that made an environmental claim, the environmental benefits were generally a secondary consideration, not a prime motivation to purchase. Price, quality, brand names and habit were much more important factors in deciding which products to buy.

The groups of ordinary shoppers were asked why they thought they did not buy more 'green' products. The reasons they gave included their lack of knowledge about which products offered these benefits. They tended to blame this on the poor display of such products in shops, and the fact that the information on environmental effects was usually in small lettering on the backs of packs. This could make green products difficult to find and they did not have the time to make the extra effort to find them. Others in these groups were aware of the existence of 'greener' products but did not think that buying them would make much difference to environmental problems.

There was also a perception that environmental messages change over time, are fashionable at different times, or that manufacturers might make a claim about one positive attribute while damaging the environment in other ways. Green products were judged to be more expensive, too. 'With environmentally friendly you always think it's more expensive' was a view that was widely held. They were also generally judged to be inferior because the make was often unknown, the packaging was found to lack impact or to be off-putting, or it was claimed to lack an ingredient, such as bleach, which was known to be effective. Some had tried green products in the past and found them to be ineffective, and others were put off by the thought that recycled products had been used before. (This was a particular worry about recycled toilet paper.)

The only factor which might encourage people in the main groups to buy more 'green products' was if the products also offered some additional personal benefit. For example, Ecover was mentioned favourably by someone who suffered from dermatitis, and organic chickens were mentioned as tasting better. Manufacturers were also perceived to have improved some products in response to legislation, such as the banning of CFCs. Washing machines were also thought to be manufactured to improved environmental standards nowadays.

Washing powder: People in the ordinary shopper groups were shown packs, leaflets about appliances and furniture, and examples of claims and symbols found during our shopping survey. When they actually looked at some of the claims on washing powders they were surprised that some brands, such as Radion and Persil, made environmental claims at all. Many of the claims were found to be confusing: some people had heard of phosphates but most were unaware of what they were or of any possible impact they might have on the environment. Few had ever heard of optical brighteners, and no one had come across zeolites, surfactants, NTA or EDTA. As a result, they tended to switch off, and to conclude that all the brands were making similar claims. A woman from one of the groups summed up this attitude to the claims on washing powders: 'I'm sure they're all trying to tell you that they are doing the same thing, but they just seem to make it so complicated. I'm sure if you read it they are all phosphate free, they've got no chlorine or bleaches and things'. (This is not true, of course, but reflects a commonly held belief.)

Paper products: The claims on these products were, by contrast, praised for their clarity and the large lettering on the front of the packs. Claims such as '100 per cent recycled' were felt to be clear and unambiguous, though people disliked claims that some recycled products contained 'low grade waste' which gave the impression that the product was inferior. They were also sceptical about one claim on a toilet paper that it did not contain wood pulp from tropical rain forests - they noted that despite the attractions of the packaging (which one group thought looked 'environmentally friendly' as it was green and featured a bird, fish, leaf and butterfly), it was not actually made from recycled paper. One group commented, 'They could go and cut down ninety per cent of Scotland, couldn't they, and use it?'. They were also confused by claims relating to bleach, optical brighteners and that some papers were 'dioxin-safe'.

Washing machines: The claims in the product literature generally related to water, detergent and energy-saving. The ordinary shoppers did not consider these to be prime considerations when choosing which make of washing machine to buy, though some people who had water meters were interested in the water-saving claims. The AEG and Bosch brochures went further than the others in that they contained a great deal of detail on their efforts to reduce the environmental impact of their manufacturing processes and on the recycling of components: although these claims impressed some, they were generally thought to be too 'remote' to influence purchasing decisions.

Fridges: The main claims related to CFCs. Since most people in our discussion groups believed these had been banned, they were surprised to read some claims to have reduced them by 50 per cent. The simpler the claim, the more it was appreciated, and several claims were criticised for trying to 'blind consumers with science' or for referring to HCFCs which no one knew about. They also queried the use of a large number of logos and symbols on fridges.

Wooden furniture: The claims expressed simply and concisely tended to be praised, but their relevance to actual purchasing decisions was questioned: 'But the thing is, if you didn't like the piece of furniture anyway, it wouldn't make you buy it, would it?'. Of all the claims, the endorsement by Friends of the Earth of Barlow Tyrie was found to be the most impressive: 'I think it's quite good because they say they're using hardwood and yet they've got the seal of approval from a substantial environmental lobbying group', commented a member of one group.

Garden products: Simplicity was again preferred in these claims. For composts, 'peat-free' was the preferred claim, though not many of the gardeners in the groups actually bought peat-free composts or mulches. Several people were sceptical of the claims that the peat was 'not harvested from areas of scientific interest'. Weed killers seemed to be a product that caused more concern than others on environmental and safety grounds. Claims such as 'biodegradable', 'organic', 'breaks down naturally in the soil' and 'harmless to the soil' were all found reassuring. There was some demand for an internationally recognised symbol to indicate that a product was safe to use. 'I find this very confusing. How do we know which of these really are

[safe]?... Somebody like the WWF or somebody in authority should give these a symbol' was a typical comment.

Paint: Most of the claims on paint were rejected. People were aware that lead had been banned from domestic paint for years, and they laughed at the claim that a paint tin contained 25 per cent recycled steel. The only claim that found favour was that a paint was water-based. This was understood to imply that the paint would be less damaging to water courses when the brushes were cleaned.

The ordinary shopper groups were asked to define some terms commonly used in environmental claims - biodegradable, environmentally friendly, recyclable, less waste, organic, safeguards natural resources and ozone friendly.

'Biodegradable' caused few problems, but people found 'environmentally friendly' much more difficult to define. It was thought to imply that the company making the claim had 'done something' or that the product is good for, or at least will not pollute, the air, soil, or ozone layer, or that it will not waste water or energy.

Although 'recycled' was a term they were all familiar with, most assumed it meant that the claim covered 100 per cent of the material used. They were surprised, or felt cheated that it could be as low as 30 per cent. The usual definition given for 'recyclable' was that the recycling will occur in the future, or that the material the product is made from 'can be used again'. Very few mentioned that the recycling might actually never happen unless initiated by the consumer.

'Organic' was correctly defined and associated mainly with vegetables. 'Less waste' caused some problems of definition as it was considered rather general. 'Ozone friendly' was another claim with which people were generally familiar, and they judged it to be important and relevant to them personally because the hole in the ozone layer could lead to increased skin cancer. Products making the claim were understood not to contain CFCs, but some associated this claim with lead-free petrol.

Most people in the groups said they thought that the claims on products were already controlled, either by trading standards, British Standards, the Advertising Standards Authority or the European Union. Within this, the more *specific* the claim, the more likely it was to be believed. They thought that specific terms such as recycled, organic, CFC-free, and biodegradable could be checked and challenged more easily. The association of such a claim with a well known manufacturer or outlet or with a tried and tested product increased its credibility. Several of the 55 logos or symbols that had been collected during the shopping survey were quite widely recognised. Symbols for long established and respected organisations such as the WWF panda and the Woodland Trust tree and the UN symbol were believed to be credible or to have some form of official status, as was the three chasing arrows symbol which was interpreted to mean recycled or recyclable.

Although people felt that the environmental aspects of products had a fairly limited effect on their purchasing behaviour, they almost all wanted environmental information to be provided on packaging and in product literature. But they stressed that the information should be presented in concise, simple language, and were particularly critical of jargon and scientific terms. They would like to see claims standardised and covered by government or European Union legislation, and a ban on trivial claims. They thought claims should only be made where there had been a genuine advance, that is, where the products or packs about which the claims are made are significantly better for the environment.

They also had some suggestions about the proliferation of symbols and logos. Not surprisingly, they thought there should be fewer. They also suggested that there should be one standardised symbol for each main aspect, in a scheme similar to the washing symbols on clothes labels. Alternatively, they favoured a symbol akin to the kitemark, which would inform the consumer that the product was certified as meeting an environmental standard. Any such symbol would, in their view, need to be protected by legislation so it could only be used when the product it covered fulfilled certain minimum requirements.

Overall, the qualitative research among 'ordinary shoppers' did not reveal the widespread 'green' shopping that some national surveys have found. It seems clear that, for many shoppers, while concern about the environment is genuine, environmental considerations fall way below price, quality, and previous experience of brands when selecting products. This seems to apply even more strongly when choosing expensive, occasional purchases such as appliances and furniture. Many shoppers had also tried green products in the past and found their performance inferior. However, when people in the groups came to assess the environmental claims made on or about products, they were clearly confused by many of the messages and by the competing claims, to the extent that they reacted against them or gave up trying to make any sense of them. They were almost unanimous in wanting coherent, consistent environmental information on products, with regulation of claims by a single competent authority.

The views of the 'light green' shoppers

If ordinary shoppers pay scant attention to the environmental claims on products, who does take any notice of these messages and logos? The recruitment for our six original groups deliberately excluded people who might have an above-average interest in, or knowledge of, environmental issues. We decided to follow up this research with an extra group discussion with more knowledgeable people - termed the 'light greens'.

Only one discussion of two hours was held, so the results have to be treated with caution. It is, however, interesting to analyse some of the differences between the light green group and the ordinary shopper groups - and the many similarities. As with the main groups, the light greens generally chose the 'greener' product option so long as other benefits - such as a keen price, a well-known brand name or that it was good for the skin - came with it. The light greens, unlike most in the main groups, were particularly keen on the presence of 'natural' ingredients. However, they would not buy green products if they failed to match up to other important considerations. Unlike the main groups, they found the so-called green detergents to be efficacious, but agreed that claims about reduced water or electricity consumption would not override brand choice when it came to buying a washing machine.

In general, the light greens were less interested in the pack appearance and more willing to experiment than the ordinary shoppers. They mentioned that conflicting messages about the environmental impact of products could discourage them from choosing green options, and could reduce the credibility of environmental claims in general. However, unlike the main groups who also picked up on this point, the light greens tended to carry on buying green products in the hope that they were doing the 'right' thing, while the ordinary shoppers gave this as a reason for sticking to their habitual choices.

Alone among all the people in our discussion groups, the light green shoppers said they did look at the ingredients listed and at the environmental information on packs when they were out shopping. However, they appeared to have no more detailed knowledge about environmental matters than the others. When pressed, they were vague about their reasons for choosing particular green products and their effects environmentally. They had no more idea than people in the main groups of what, for example, phosphates or zeolites are, and why these or bleach might be bad for the environment, other than that they 'end up in rivers'. Also, despite their claim that they do tend to look at packaging, they were only spontaneously aware of a very few more claims than people in the main groups, recognised no more symbols, and were just as likely to be confused by the various claims and symbols shown to them.

The light greens were more interested than those in the main groups in examining the claims made on packs and seemed to be more critical of some of them. They were also more impressed than the ordinary shoppers by claims relating to the manufacture of the product and the recycling of components. In general they were more interested in environmental issues in the wider sense than the general public and were more likely to be impressed by more types of environmental claim. Otherwise, many of their other views accorded with the main groups, particularly on the status and credibility of claims and symbols, and their recommendations for action.

Conclusions

Our research seems to suggest that many, perhaps most, people do not pay much attention to the detailed information given in environmental claims on products, but that they are keen to have the information. When pressed, in the artificial conditions of a group discussion, people in all the groups certainly found the information given confusing and at times were misled by it. In our view, the information provided with or on a product is not just a marketing activity but is, or should be regarded as, part of the delivery of the product. As such, consumers have a right to expect it to be honest and truthful. Indeed, it should be in the interest of the companies making the claims for it to be so.

Other public policy considerations, though beyond the scope of this paper, are also relevant in the wider context of environmental claims. The UK has undertaken to meet certain national and international targets concerned with the reduction of pollution, the minimisation of waste and the more efficient use of energy. Environmental statements about products may have a role to play in achieving these targets. Moreover the scepticism, revealed by our research, with which consumers now view some of the environmental claims on products devalues the achievement of truly innovative breakthroughs. Such scepticism will discourage those manufacturers who are genuinely trying to reduce the harmful environmental impact of their products from making statements about it.

6. The views of manufacturers and retailers

As part of the extensive consultation exercise we carried out for this investigation we wrote to twelve large retailers, three industry groupings concerned with the environment, and four other industrial companies that make some products promoted on the basis of their environmental attributes. We were particularly interested to hear their views on the workings of the current legislation in the context of environmental claims, any opinions they might have on whether and how the legislation could be changed, and what such changes might cost.

In the event, very few responded formally, though subsequent telephone contact and further correspondence did elicit a few more comments. However, we were not able to obtain any views on the likely costs of improved mechanisms for dealing with dubious environmental claims. This summary of views is therefore based not just on the consultation but also on published statements by some of the retailers concerned.

The views of retailers

It is clear that retailers have divergent views on the use and abuse of environmental claims. Several leading retailers, among them J. Sainsbury and Tesco, expressed their opposition to increased regulation or to changes in the Trade Descriptions Act. Sainsbury's commented, 'We would advocate that no change is necessary to the Trade Descriptions Act, but that more effective enforcement be achieved in the area of "green claims" ' [J. Sainsbury, letter to the NCC, 31 July 1995]. Some other retailers would not be averse to a change in the law. Marks and Spencer commented: 'with the concern that existing law might not be effective, either the Trade Descriptions Act should be amended or a specific Bill be promulgated to clarify what should be allowed and disallowed' [Marks and Spencer, letter to the NCC, 5 June 1995]. The

Body Shop, the Co-op and Kingfisher plc were among the sponsors of a private member's bill, the Environmental Claims Bill, in the 1994 parliament whose effect would have been to amend the Trade Descriptions Act to make clear that it covers environmental claims, and to require manufacturers and retailers to substantiate product claims.

Sainsbury's is of the opinion that current legislation could be used more effectively against misleading environmental claims. For their part, they try to monitor and police the environmental claims made on all the products sold within their stores. This approach is also adopted by Marks and Spencer, for whom such monitoring is more easily achieved as they sell only their own brand. 'For our part, we use only sparingly any overt "environmental messages" on our products. In response to the concern over the use of CFC propellants, we marked our aerosols "CFC free"...' [Marks and Spencer, letter to the NCC, 5 June 1995].

The Co-op sent us details of the detailed guidelines they issue to suppliers on the use of environmental claims on the Co-op brands. Expressions such as 'environment friendly' are banned, and the emphasis is put on factual claims addressed to the informed consumer, with as full an explanation as possible. Claims also have to relate to a genuine improvement either compared with the previous formulation or with the industry norm.

Other retailers also regulate claims on products in their shops. B&Q told us they had decided to remove all claims from timber products in 1991 because 'in the absence of a claim with both credibility and integrity, it was better to have no claim at all' [B&Q, letter to the NCC, 28 July 1995]. B&Q are working towards the establishment of a certification and labelling scheme for all timber products, but accept this may not be relevant for all products.

The views of manufacturers and trade associations

As with the retailers, those few manufacturers and trade associations who responded to our consultation were divided as to whether current legislation was effective. Most also stated that they made few environmental claims. SmithKline Beecham think that the existing controls may be adequate but possibly not well known or well enforced. The company 'makes virtually no environmental claims because it is aware of the difficulties involved and the many controls that exist, but misleading environmental claims are still to be seen in the market place, often made by smaller or less knowledgeable companies, and the aim should be to minimise these' [SmithKline Beecham, letter to the NCC, 3 July 1995].

The Pulp and Paper Information Centre (PPIC), which is responsible for the communications activities of the four main trade associations for the paper industry, sent us a helpful leaflet they publish which tries to explain to consumers the differences between the environmental labels and marketing logos commonly found on paper. The PPIC deals with around a thousand enquiries a month from both consumers and industry seeking clarification of environmental claims. They commented that 'guidelines for companies wishing to make environmental claims are probably as necessary as protection for the consumer' [PPIC, letter to the NCC, 29 August 1995].

One trade association which produces guidelines for its members on environmental claims is the Soap and Detergent Industry Association (SDIA). The SDIA is in favour of amending the Trade Descriptions Act to make it clear that it covers environmental claims. It is particularly concerned about on-pack claims which are not subject to the controls on advertising operated through the advertising codes. The SDIA has a written policy on environmental affairs and guidelines for negative ingredient claims (issued in February 1990). The guidelines state that manufacturers should never flag the absence of an ingredient which is not present in any significant brands in the category. When flagging the absence of an ingredient which is used in some other brands, this should be presented as neutral information. So a product without phosphates should be described as containing 'zero or nil phosphates' rather than 'phosphate-free'. Finally, the guidelines tell manufacturers never to use advertising copy to impugn the human or environmental safety of well-established ingredients used in other brands [SDIA, letter to the NCC, 28 July, 1995]. The SDIA told us it has acted to enforce its guidelines, by contacting 'a number of companies in our industry who have made, in our view, dubious environmental claims and requested them to change'. In one case, in 1989, the Association was unable to resolve the issue during discussions with one company and, when the claims were repeated in advertisements, referred it to the Advertising Standards Authority, which upheld the complaint (see chapter 8).

Another industry association which responded to our consultation was the Alliance for Beverage Cartons and the Environment. This is a coalition of companies that produce paperboard and make drinks cartons and so is mainly concerned with environmental claims about packaging. Its main recommendation is that there should be 'strong encouragement for all those making environmental claims to make sure the claims are honest'. The Alliance would like this to be non-statutory. 'The Alliance practice in the UK has evolved in a non-statutory climate, and we are satisfied with that climate' [Alliance for Beverage Cartons and the Environment, letter to the NCC, 26 July 1995].

Respondents who favoured a non-statutory solution had a number of suggestions as to how the enforcement of existing rules on green claims could be made more effective. These included the development of industry codes of practice, which would provide guidance on best practice and a consistent basis for court decisions, and which could take the arbitrary nature out of a range of subjective interpretations of the current legislation. They pointed out that leading companies have a strong incentive to develop and keep to sound environmental principles because they stand to lose too much if their credibility and reputation is undermined. They also suggested that the drafting of British Standards on environmental claims would help to establish best practice, and that the policing of the legislation would be helped by a government information campaign to raise public awareness and publicise the existence of industry codes, once they had been agreed.

Some of the possible legal solutions are explored in more detail in chapter 11. Chapter 9 explores in more depth accreditation, approval schemes and the role of standards. We look at the possible use of voluntary codes of practice at the end of chapter 8.

7. How green claims are regulated

Environmental claims currently fall within three different forms of regulation. These are the controls on print and broadcast advertising, the control of the Trade Descriptions Act 1968 on on-pack claims, and the Department of Trade and Industry-sponsored voluntary code on non-advertising green claims. This means that the existing controls encompass three types of regulation: self-regulation with statutory backing enforceable through civil action; regulation by statute with criminal sanctions for infringement; and wholly voluntary regulation via a code. In this chapter we outline the three types of regulation. In the next chapter we assess how they work in practice.

Claims through advertising

Most of the non-broadcast advertising that appears in this country is regulated by the advertising industry itself, through its codes of practice. These codes, though voluntary in their application, have been given statutory backing through the Control of Misleading Advertising Regulations 1988. Broadcast advertising is treated differently. Complaints about broadcast advertisements are not handled by the Advertising Standards Authority, but by the broadcasting authorities themselves. Radio and television advertising is subject to a dual system of control. All scripts of advertisements which make environmental claims must be vetted and cleared by the Broadcast Advertising Clearance Centre (BACC), which operates specific rules on how and where claims may be made and, on transmission, are subject to the Radio Authority and Independent Television Commission rules on environmental claims.

The Control of Misleading Advertising Regulations came into force in June 1988 implementing a European Union directive. Under the regulations, the Director General of Fair Trading is required to consider complaints about misleading advertisements and marketing claims other than those on commercial radio or television. Before he considers a complaint, the Director General may require the complainant to try other established means of resolving it and show that the complaint has not been dealt with adequately. This is designed to ensure that the existing channels for complaints about advertising are used first - namely, the Advertising Standards Authority which polices the codes on advertising and sales promotion, and local authority trading standards departments which are responsible for bringing prosecutions under the relevant consumer legislation.

In practice, the Director General deals with very few cases. The Advertising Standards Authority say they have referred just nine cases to him. In dealing with any complaints about a misleading advertisement, the Director General of Fair Trading is required to take account of all the interests involved, particularly the public interest, and the desirability of encouraging the control of advertisements by self-regulatory bodies. In practice, it seems that both the Director General and the Advertising Standards Authority are happy to leave most cases to be dealt with by the ASA, and it is only persistent flouting of ASA rulings which will induce the Director General to take action.

If he thinks that an advertisement referred to him is misleading, the Director General may seek an injunction to prevent the advertisement from being published. If he needs to act before all the facts can be presented to a court, he may apply for an interlocutory injunction. Before granting an injunction, the court must be satisfied that the advertisement is misleading and take account of all the interests involved, particularly the public interest. In considering an application for an injunction, the court may require the advertiser to substantiate the accuracy of any factual claim being made. The Director General does not have to prove that actual harm has been caused by the advertisement's publication nor that there was an intention to mislead. By July 1995, the Director General had yet to deal with a complaint concerning environmental claims in advertisements [Office of Fair Trading, letter to the NCC, 31 July 1995].

Two features of the regulations on advertising are of particular interest. The first is the central importance of a voluntary code of practice which is backed up by statutory authority. This was emphasised in an early decision to grant an interlocutory injunction under the Regulations. In *Director General of Fair Trading v Tobyward Ltd* (1989) [2 All ER 266], Mr Justice Hoffman commented '… the regulations contemplate that there will only be intervention by the director when the voluntary system has failed. It is in my judgement desirable and in accordance with the public interest to which I must have regard that the courts should support the principle of self-regulation. I think that advertisers would be more inclined to accept the rulings of their self-regulatory bodies if it were generally known that in cases in which their procedures had been exhausted and the advertiser was still publishing an advertisement which appeared to be prima facie misleading an injunction would ordinarily be granted'.

The second striking feature of the controls on advertising is the requirement for advertisers to be in a position to substantiate factual claims. This is a feature of the codes themselves. The British Codes of Advertising and Sales Promotion, which are the codes adjudicated by the Advertising Standards Authority, state that 'before submitting an advertisement for publication, advertisers must hold documentary evidence to prove all claims, whether direct or implied, that are capable of objective substantiation' [British Codes of Advertising and Sales Promotion, February 1995, point 3.1]. For broadcast advertising, the requirements for substantiation of claims are similar. The Control of Misleading Advertising Regulations vest the statutory duty to consider complaints about misleading broadcast advertising in the Independent Television Commission and the Radio Authority. These bodies also set and enforce the standards to which broadcast advertisers must adhere in their respective codes. Under both codes, an advertiser is always required to substantiate any factual claim made for a product [Broadcast Advertising Clearance Centre, *Notes of Guidance for Broadcast Advertising*, 1994, para 1.1.15].

So the Advertising Standards Authority forms the core of controls over advertising claims in the non-broadcast media. It was established in 1962 to provide independent scrutiny of the then newly-created system of self-regulation set up by the advertising industry. It is a limited company, and at least half of its twelve-member governing council is unconnected with the advertising business [British Codes of Advertising and Sales Promotion, February 1995, paras 68.11 and 68.12]. It is financed by a voluntary levy on display advertising, which is raised by the advertising industry through the Advertising Board of Finance. The latter body acts as a go-between, masking the identities of those who actually pay the levy from the ASA and thereby guaranteeing its impartiality. The ASA costs about £2.5 million a year to run [ASA, *Annual Report*, 1993].

The ASA codes apply to advertisements in newspapers, magazines, brochures, leaflets, circulars, mailings, catalogues, faxes, posters, aerial announcements, cinema and video commercials, viewdata services, advertising and sales promotions, and mailing lists to consumers. They do not cover broadcast commercials (covered by the Independent Television Commission and the Radio Authority), classified private advertisements, flyposting, oral communications including telephone calls, press releases, and packages, wrappers and labels unless they advertise a sales promotion or are visible in an advertisement. Neither do they cover point of sales displays, except for those covered by the Code on Sales Promotion and the Cigarette Code [British Code of Advertising and Sales Promotion, February 1995, para 1.2]. An advertising claim covered by the code can be implied, direct, written, spoken or visual.

The codes are constantly under review, and have been extended several times. The ASA has also taken over responsibility for areas of advertising activity which have developed since it was founded in 1962. For instance, in 1992, after a lengthy period of consultation within the industry, the ASA took over responsibility for the monitoring and complaints procedures in direct marketing, the fastest growing sector of the advertising industry [Advertising Association, *Annual Report*, 1993].

The Advertising Standards Authority, the Radio Authority and the Independent Television Commission all have specific codes on the use of environmental claims in advertising. These have been developed in response to the increased use of environmental claims in advertising since the late 1980s. The ASA issued its first guidance note on the subject in 1990. This was updated in 1994 and formed the basis of the current rules on environmental claims in the British Codes of Advertising and Sales Promotion (see appendix 5). The Radio Authority Advertising Code has contained a section on environmental claims since its inception in January 1991. Similar codes are operated by the Independent Television Commission, and the Broadcast Advertising Clearance Centre (BACC) which vets advertising that is to be broadcast nationally or regionally.

On-pack claims

On-pack claims fall under the control of the Trade Descriptions Act 1968, which deals with false and misleading descriptions of goods and services. Section 1 establishes that it is a criminal offence to apply a false trade description to any goods, and to supply or offer to supply goods to which a false trade description is applied. Section 2 lists the categories which constitute a trade description. These include an indication of the quantity or size; of the method of manufacture; of the product's composition, fitness for purpose, strength, behaviour, performance or accuracy and any other physical characteristics; that the product has been tested or approved by any person; the place or date of manufacture and by whom, and other history, including previous use or ownership. They do not specifically mention environmental claims, for the simple reason that the legislation pre-dates such concerns.

Section 3 defines a false trade description as one which is false to a material degree. The test seems to be 'What would an ordinary man understand by the description and to what degree would he be misled by it?' (see Richard Bragg, *Trade Descriptions*, Oxford University Press, 1991, p. 43). However, the description itself need not be false provided that it is sufficiently misleading to the ordinary person. Section 3(3) also catches symbols which convey a certain impression and are therefore 'likely to be taken as indication of the matters specified' in section 2. Section 7 and section 9, which have never been used, give the Minister for Corporate and Consumer Affairs powers to make orders assigning definite meanings to expressions used in trade descriptions and in advertisements.

The Act is enforced by local authority trading standards departments which have the power to bring prosecutions under the criminal law, with the strict rules of evidence that apply in such cases. So it is up to the prosecution to prove the case beyond all reasonable doubt. In practice, this has led to heavy reliance on the use of expert witnesses and scientific testing in the area of product claims. In general, however, trading standards officers have found the Act a useful and effective means of dealing with false and misleading product claims (see chapter 8).

Non-advertising green claims

Environmental claims described as 'non-advertising green claims' are the subject of a voluntary code of practice which was published by the Department of Trade and Industry in April 1994. The claims referred to are general marketing claims not covered by the Advertising Standards Authority. These are taken to include corporate identity campaigns, corporate advertising, company reports, educational literature, leaflets and promotional videos. Some of these categories do in fact overlap with the ASA's activities. The code is based on the International Chamber of Commerce model code on environmental advertising, and incorporates a statement of principles which it would like to encourage people to adopt. It is difficult to evaluate the effectiveness of this code, which rather depends on it being widely known, as there is no monitoring system in place which could assess how widespread is compliance with the code.

8. How effective is the regulation?

Advertising

We wrote to all the leading advertising organisations to ask for their views on how the current system of regulation deals with environmental claims. Replies were received from the Independent Television Commission, the Broadcast Advertising Clearance Centre, the Advertising Standards Authority, the Radio Authority, the Incorporated Society of British Advertisers, the Advertising Association, and the Institute of Practitioners in Advertising. None of the other organisations we consulted commented on the regulations on advertising.

According to the Incorporated Society of British Advertisers (ISBA), there are no types of environmental claim which may not be covered by existing controls. This view is supported by the Institute of Practitioners in Advertising (IPA), which also maintains that 'in the field of advertising, the statutory controls through the ITC and the self regulatory controls through the ASA work reasonably well, and they have become increasingly more effective as the experience of the issues has grown over the years' [IPA, letter to the NCC, 10 August 1995]. The ISBA concludes that 'environmental claims in advertising seem to be totally suitable for the present system of self-regulation which is quickly able to adapt to changing circumstances' [ISBA, letter to the NCC, 27 July 1995].

The section of the non-broadcast advertising code which deals with environmental claims is in appendix 5. All the broadcast and non-broadcast advertising codes are broadly similar, but one potentially significant difference is in how they deal with very general, non-specific claims, such as 'environmentally friendly'. The Broadcast Advertising Clearance Centre guidance simply considers these claims to be unlikely as they require substantiation on a 'cradle to grave basis'. 'Since on this basis' it states, 'practically all products have some impact on the environment, categorical statements such as "environment friendly", "safe" or "green" are unlikely to be appropriate to any mass-produced product'.

The ASA code, on the other hand, does allow for the possibility that a manufactured product may be 'environmentally friendly', a point hotly disputed by most environmental organisations. Rule 49.2 states that 'claims such as "environmentally friendly" or "wholly biodegradable" should not be used without qualification, *unless advertisers can provide convincing evidence that their product will cause no environmental damage'*.

In practice, however, the complaints the ASA has investigated over the last five years do not seem to indicate that this has posed a problem yet. Seven complaints about products which made absolute statements about their favourable environmental impact were upheld over this period. Examples included a poster advertisement for Kyocera printers tagged as 'the world's first environment-friendly page printers'. In its ruling the ASA stated that an absolute claim was unacceptable, though the documentation supplied by the company showed that the product was significantly less damaging to the environment than other models [*ASA Monthly Report*, September 1993].

Similarly, three claims by advertisers on the environmental benefits of diesel fuel and cars were upheld by the ASA in October and November 1993. In one claim that diesel cars 'do their bit to help save the planet' the ASA ruled that, in order to avoid the implication that diesel was *beneficial* as opposed to *less harmful* to the environment (the presumed comparison being with catalyst-equipped petrol-engined cars), the claim should have been fully qualified, to indicate the specified pollutants it was comparing [*ASA Monthly Report*, October 1993]. In another case, in November 1993, the ASA stated that an advertisement went too far in implying that diesel was an environmental benefit when it referred to the 'obvious environmental benefits of diesel'. In a similar ruling, a statement that diesel fuel was environmentally friendly due to lower levels of harmful emissions was not permitted, because the ASA was concerned 'that a product which resulted in any amount of smoke or emissions was described as friendly rather than less harmful to the environment' [*ASA Monthly Report*, October 1993].

We have yet to find a case where the ASA has ruled that a product was 'environmentally friendly'. However, if these claims in advertisements are not challenged, they may continue, because the ASA acts on receipt of a complaint and problems are therefore dealt with retrospectively. The ASA will, however, advise on the wording to be used in an advertisement before it is published, and many agencies do seek such advice.

The ASA has also ruled on some environmental claims on detergents similar to the claims which people who participated in our market research found confusing (see chapter 5). In this fiercely competitive market, the leading companies monitor each other's advertisements closely and complain to the ASA if they find something they are not happy with in their competitors' claims. One example of a complaint to the ASA about detergent advertising was by Lever about Reckitt & Colman's Down to Earth washing up liquid and concentrated automatic washing liquid [*ASA Monthly Report*, March 1994]. The details of one case emphasise the importance the ASA attaches to comparative claims. The wording complained of was 'our washing up liquid ... looks after rivers. We get independent experts to conduct stringent tests for biodegradability, on the whole product, to ensure we're reducing the harm to the environment'. Lever complained that the implication was that competitors' products were less biodegradable and did more harm to the environment. The advertisers denied the claim was comparative. But the ASA decided that it was and, as the advertisers were unable to show that their products were less harmful to the environment, the complaint was upheld.

A further complaint, on the automatic washing liquid in the same product range, objected to the wording in the advertisement which stated that the product 'uses citrates ... these citrates replace phosphates which can harm aquatic life'. Lever objected to the implication that competing automatic liquids contained phosphates, and the ASA upheld the complaint as it understood the vast majority of washing liquids did not contain phosphates.

Another, much earlier complaint about advertisements for 'green' detergents was made by the industry's trade body, the Soap and Detergent Industry Association (SDIA) in 1989. It objected to some wording of claims on the pack of Ecover detergent and, when the claims were repeated as a leaflet distributed in shops and so fell within the code on advertising, the SDIA picked three sample claims and referred them to the ASA in June 1989. The claims were quite complicated, but all referred to the absence of ingredients - petroleum based detergents, NTA and EDTA, and optical brighteners, and in the case of the last three, their harmful effects. The SDIA's complaint was upheld on the grounds that Ecover had failed to substantiate the harmful effects of EDTA and optical brighteners. The ASA also ruled that Ecover should avoid giving the impression that NTA was likely to be found in competitors' products, and that one of the non-ionic surfactants used by Ecover was petroleum based, and so they should describe the composition of their products more fully when making claims [*ASA Case Report*, October 1990]. The company was asked to change the wording in its leaflet, but this ruling did not, of course, apply to or affect claims on the product itself [SDIA, letter to the NCC, 28 July 1995].

Many of the ASA rulings have been controversial and subject to strong criticism by advertisers and complainants. During the course of our review, for example, the ASA declined to take action against Elida Gibbs for their advertising campaign for Organics shampoo, which the Soil Association considered to be in breach of the code by making implied and unsubstantiated environmental claims. The issue here was that 'organic' has ten different dictionary definitions, and the company convinced the ASA that it was not using the word in such a way as to imply that the product contained ingredients from organic farms, but in a totally different sense. This interpretation is fiercely disputed by the Soil Association and others.

The fact remains that the number of environmental claims of a dubious nature that appear in advertisements appears to have declined substantially since the codes were tightened and made specifically applicable to environmental claims, while the evidence from our survey suggests that similar claims on products, which are not covered by the ASA codes, are still fairly widespread.

Product descriptions

Product descriptions on the product itself and on leaflets designed to accompany products come under the scrutiny of trading standards officers when seeking to enforce the Trade Descriptions Act. It was thought for some time that environmental claims on products were not actually covered by the Act, as they are not listed in section 2. There have, however, been some successful prosecutions of companies making environmental claims on products under the Act.

The Local Authorities Co-ordinating Body on Food and Trading Standards (LACOTS) has asked to be informed of all successful prosecutions of environmental claims. To date they have received reports of four cases, the outlines of which are shown in the table on the next page. They, and we, have found no others, but as there is no central systematic collection and reporting of such cases, this is not conclusive evidence that there have been none. Four successful cases is a very small number, given the time scale and the wide variety of such claims on products. Even if LACOTS has been informed of only a quarter of the total of such cases, the strike rate would still be very low.

Successful prosecutions of environmental claims

Case	Date of offence	Company	Claim	Authority/Court	Reason claim false	Wording of offence/offence	Fine
A.R.M. Marketing Ltd	8.5.89	A.R.M. Marketing Ltd., 11-13 Waterloo Place, Leamington Spa, Warwickshire CB32	'Biodegradable'	Surrey County Council Gadstone Magistrates (Dorking)	The involatile, insoluble nature of the material would make it slow to disperse and degrade unless emulsified	Contrary to section 1(1)(b) Trade Descriptions Act 1968	£500 guilty plea
Addis Ltd	3.10.90	Addis Ltd., Brushworks, Ware Road, Hertford Herts	'Ozone friendly'	L.B. Merton Wimbledon Magistrates	The fire extinguisher contained an extinguishing agent, halon 1211, a well-known ozone depleter	Supplying domestic fire extinguisher falsely described as ozone friendly; contrary to section 1(1)(b) Trade Descriptions Act 1968	2 x £1,400 = £2,800
Asda Stores Ltd.	14.3.91	Asda Stores Ltd., Asda House, Southbank, Great Wilson St., Leeds LS11 5AD	'Environment friendly - all ASDA meat and poultry trays are ozone friendly. They are produced without CFCs, which is alleged to damage the earth's ozone layer'	Warwickshire County Council	The tray was made with the use of CFCs	Contrary to section 1(1)(b) Trade Descriptions Act 1968	2 x £1,500 = £3,000
Halfords Ltd.	18.4.91	Spectra Brands plc, Treloggan Industrial Estate, Newquay, Cornwall, TR7 2SX	'Ozone friendly'	Norfolk County Council Norwich Magistrates	The canister contained 111-trichloroethane, an ozone-depleting gas	Contrary to section 1(1)(a) Trade Descriptions Act 1968	£500

(source: LACOTS, 1995)

Several explanations for this low level of activity have been suggested. One is that trading standards officers do not have the confidence to use the existing legislation because they do not think that environmental claims are covered by the Act. The argument is that, because of this, they do not want to waste time and resources on prosecutions which they feel would have no likelihood of success. Another explanation is that environmental claims cause particular problems with standards of proof. As the onus is on the prosecution to prove the case and as many claims are quite vague, non-specific and ill-defined, it may be that trading standards officers find it difficult to accumulate sufficient expert evidence to stand up in court. A third problem may be with the legislation itself. Is it really the appropriate means to deal with misleading environmental claims?

An examination of the four cases on which we have details does not shed much light on whether the Trade Descriptions Act does or does not cover environmental claims. It is possible that the defendants argued, unsuccessfully, that it does not, but the fact that the prosecutions were successful and there were no appeals rather gives the lie to this line of argument. However, it could be argued that claims framed in such a way as to relate solely to the *impact* of the goods upon the environment (such as ozone friendly), as opposed to the *method of manufacture* and all those things listed in section 2 of the Act (see chapter 7), are not actually covered. Notwithstanding the fact that the prosecutions were successful against Addis and Halfords (see the table), we have been given legal advice that these sorts of claim may not in fact be covered. The only way to make sure of this would probably be to amend section 2 and add a new paragraph to the list of definitions of a trade description, to cover a statement about the impact of a product (or the way it is processed, manufactured or distributed) on the environment.

In terms of whether it is difficult to get evidence or not, the cases do provide some insight. Two of the cases relate to claims about the absence of ozone-depleting gases, which are readily proved or disproved by chemical analysis. The other two claims are also factual, although unfortunately we have no further details of how the trading standards departments proved their cases. Presumably either the tray in question was or was not made with the use of CFCs, and expert evidence was available on this, or the company pleaded guilty. Similarly, with the one case on biodegradability, the company pleaded guilty, but expert evidence must have been on hand to support the case. In neither of these two cases does it seem likely that there was conflicting expert opinion. This still leaves open the difficult question as to how bad for the environment a product must be before a hyperbolic statement, or 'puff' in lawyers' language, becomes 'false to a material degree' within the terms of the Act. Our legal advice is that if the product is no worse than average, the statement will not be false to a material degree.

In the course of our review, we have tried to collect examples of unsuccessful prosecutions of environmental claims under the Act, in an attempt to throw light on why there have been so few successful ones reported. By their very nature, it is extremely difficult to get information about prosecutions that have failed. The only information we have managed to obtain is about four cases brought in Walsall in 1990 and a case in Warwickshire.

The Walsall cases were brought against four different companies - SmithKline Beecham, Colgate Palmolive, Superdrug and Boots the Chemist - and all concerned aerosols which had replaced CFCs with hydrocarbons as a propellant. Three of the claims prosecuted used identical wording, namely 'environmentally friendly'. The fourth used the claim 'environmentally friendly - CFC-free'. The Council trading standards department decided to bring prosecutions on all four cases on the grounds that the alternative propellant, while not a CFC, was still harmful to the environment and so the product could not be described as 'environmentally friendly'. An expert witness was found who gave a comprehensive statement on the effects of hydrocarbons on the atmosphere. The effect on the upper atmosphere was nil but, because the aerosols contained volatile organic compounds, namely hydrocarbons, which were a contributory factor to low-level ozone and hence to smog, they were harmful to the environment.

When the first case was brought, however, the expert admitted under cross-examination that, as a scientist, he could not be one hundred per cent certain of the effect of CFCs on the upper atmosphere, and that no scientist would ever say he was sure about the lower atmosphere. As a result, the case collapsed. Also, though the case did not get on to this, the defence sought to cast doubt on the environmental impact of the use of one aerosol and whether it was sufficient to make its description as 'environmentally friendly' false to a material degree under the terms of the Act. Walsall were advised that the four cases were unlikely to succeed and agreed to drop them.

The failure of these cases is well known in the trading standards world. It highlights some of the difficulties in bringing prosecutions. It is difficult to find an expert who is both impartial (in this case it had to be someone who had never worked for one of the four companies and might never want to work for them in the future) and can withstand the rigours of cross-examination. Scientific evidence may be very hard to come by, expensive and, given that most good scientists are sceptics, lack the certainty to sustain the burden of proof in a criminal case on its own. The final problem centres on local authority trading standards departments themselves. They are notoriously under-resourced and simply cannot risk losing cases where the law and the facts are not absolutely clear-cut.

The Warwickshire case concerned an 'organic flour' which, analysis in 1989 confirmed, contained pesticide residues. Although these were within the levels permitted by food regulations, the trading standards department contended that food described as 'organic' would not be expected to contain any pesticide residue. Flours not described as organic were also tested and found not to contain any detectable levels of pesticide. The defence argued that the description organic referred to the method of production, and was not a guarantee that the product was free of pesticide residue which could have been in the soil for many years or contaminated the crop while in storage or by spraydrift. The defence were supported in this argument by the Soil Association and a board member of the UK Register of Organic Food Standards (UKROFS), and the argument was accepted by the magistrates.

Since this case, the EU directive on organic food production has been implemented. The regulations state that the description does refer to the methods of food production laid down in the directive, and do not require testing for residues. Warwickshire has concluded that, although it lost the case on the facts, the publicity it generated informed people that organic food can contain pesticide residues. It has noticed that since then organisations and traders have ceased to claim that organic food is pesticide free [Warwickshire Trading Standards, letter to the NCC, 2 November 1995]. The incident shows how difficult it is to bring a prosecution when opinions as to the definition of terms used in environmental claims vary.

The Local Authorities Co-ordinating Body on Food and Trading Standards (LACOTS) submitted a long memorandum on environmental claims in response to our consultation for this review. As an organisation, it has done a great deal of work on the subject and produced a model leaflet on environmental claims for local authorities to use. LACOTS believes that the Trade Descriptions Act is 'an effective and unburdensome control on misleading claims' and the fact that it can be used for environmental claims is shown by the successful prosecutions. The difficulty faced in enforcing it in this area relates, in its view, to the subjective or unprovable nature of many claims.

Straightforward claims about the absence of particular chemicals are fairly readily challenged, as in some of the successful prosecutions outlined above. Harder to deal with under the legislation are claims such as 'no CFCs' which, while true, omit to mention other relevant information, such as that the product never used CFCs or that the CFCs that were in it have been replaced by a chemical known to have a different but still detrimental effect on the environment. Other claims which cause problems are those on the production, impact or derivation of products. Only the manufacturer, who is also the person making the claim, is likely to know if a bench is made from 'wood from a sustainable source'. LACOTS comments that in this case 'there is no obligation on him to demonstrate the accuracy of the claim, and without information from him it is unlikely that any court could be convinced beyond any reasonable doubt' [LACOTS, letter to the NCC, 31 July 1995]. Another problem is with claims which do not actually describe the environmental benefit to be derived from buying the product, but simply try to promote a green image. 'Environmentally friendly' falls into this category, as do such claims as 'made with care for the environment' and 'environmentally responsible'. Again, the onus is on the prosecution to demonstrate convincingly that these statements are false.

As we have seen already, retailers appear to be divided in their views on whether the Trade Descriptions Act is sufficient to control environmental claims on products. Sainsbury's took the view, in its response to us, that it needs to be enforced more effectively. Marks and Spencer said that it believes trading standard standards officers 'have insufficient confidence to use it in this connection'. Other retailers, although they did not respond to our consultation, have taken a different line, and three were among the original sponsors of the Environmental Claims Bill in 1993.

LACOTS rejects the suggestion that trading standards officers have been timid in pursuit of misleading environmental claims. It points out to us that many local authorities have strong environmental policies and that there is some pressure on trading standards officers to bring prosecutions on misleading environmental claims. Overall, the Trade Descriptions Act is generally acknowledged to have worked well as a piece of consumer legislation (although there are parts of it, outside the terms of this review, which the National Consumer Council has long wished to tidy up). As it stands, however, the Act is clearly unable to deal with many dubious environmental claims at present.

In particular, it is virtually impossible to take action on claims that are unverifiable, such as claims about the sources of a product and some compositional claims; on claims that, though true, are meaningless in a wider sense, such as the claimed absence of an ingredient which most competing products do not contain either; on claims that are narrowly true but mask a wider falsehood, such as that the product does not contain one ingredient harmful to the environment while silently containing others that are; on claims that are true but are also true for all products in the class; on claims which lack any accepted definitions; and on vague and woolly hyperbolic claims - 'mere puffs' - that are impossible to prove or disprove. Many environmental claims fall into these categories. In its present form, the Trade Descriptons Act is too narrowly drawn and restrictive to deal with these.

Non-advertising green claims

General environmental marketing claims not covered by the Advertising Standards Association are the subject of a voluntary code of pratice sponsored by the Department of Trade and Industry. It is very difficult to judge whether this code is effective in the absence of any monitoring system.

A very recent study looked at one of the areas the guidelines cover [Sutton Trading Standards, *Non-Advertising Green Claims: An evaluation into the use of green claims made as part of corporate environmental image building*, December 1995]. The author of the study collected brochures, leaflets and reports from a range of organisations in the public and private sectors over a nine-month period and looked at any claim made relating to the publication of the document.

The study found twenty-three ways of expressing concern for the environment while making a claim about the paper on which it was printed. Claims ranged from the wholly vague 'this Report and Accounts is printed on paper designed to take into account the total environmental impact' (Welsh Water plc), via the unsubstantiated 'text, pages and covers made from environmentally friendly paper' (DTI Guide for Businesses), to the over-complex, such as 'printed on Recyconomic Coated 70gsm 10c/90d, a paper made from 100 per cent post-consumer printed and unprinted waste' (National Trust). Of the twenty-three claims, the study concludes that over one-third (nine) clearly did not comply with the guidelines, nearly half (eleven) were ambiguous or expressed in terms that would be difficult for the average person to understand, and only three were relatively clear, simple statements of fact. One example of good practice was the UK Eco-Labelling Board Bulletin which stated that it was 'printed on recycled paper using non-toxic inks'.

The study notes that the guidelines state that claims should provide accurate and meaningful information, that claims should be fully and demonstrably substantiated, and should not be ambiguous and vague. Unfortunately, very few of the claims they found met these requirements, and the study concludes that there is widespread non-compliance with the guidelines in the area they looked at.

Voluntary industry codes of practice

Voluntary industry codes of practice can be issued by the industry or by the industry in partnership with the Office of Fair Trading. Under section 124 of the Fair Trading Act 1973, the Office of Fair Trading (OFT) can issue codes of practice after they have been drawn up by voluntary agreement with particular sectors under the OFT's supervision. In the past, these were sometimes initiated by the OFT when a particular consumer problem - such as a high and persistent level of customer complaints - about a whole sector had been identified which did not merit legislation, or where it was thought legislation would not be effective. There are none which cover environmental claims and no new codes have been issued for several years. The problems are that they may not be well publicised, so that consumers do not know of their existence, and the OFT does not have the resources to monitor their application in practice. Voluntary codes tend to be respected by the virtuous and ignored by the rogues. If they are not monitored for compliance, it is impossible to judge whether they are being effective.

If it was decided to regulate environmental claims through industry codes of practice, the first problem would be to establish an effective system for monitoring claims and some sort of body to report to. It might be argued that trading standards officers would be able to undertake monitoring as part of their regular work, but they could only be expected to undertake this if they were confident that complaints would be passed on and dealt with, and that the wording of the codes was authoritative and effective.

Industry codes of practice, where they exist, are generally administered by trade associations. Their level of resources and extent to which their membership covers the industry varies enormously. So do their aims and objectives. Some see their role as purely defensive, to protect the interests of their members (who, after all, pay their bills). Others have a more educational and informational role. And some specialise in the technical aspects of their particular industry. It is extremely difficult to see how such a disparate group of organisations could provide the necessary credibility and consistency in dealing with environmental claims urged by so many of our consultees. Nor are they necessarily going to win the confidence of trading standards officers and the general public.

In order to be credible and effective, voluntary codes of practice have to aim for high standards. If they were to be adopted on an industry by industry basis, it would be essential that they use similar wording, adapted to the particular case of each industry. Otherwise they would quickly turn into an enforcement nightmare. The standards would have to be at least as high as, probably higher than, current legislation. The International Chamber of Commerce code on environmental advertising (see appendix 6) or the Advertising Standards Authority's code (see appendix 5) might be taken as models. Taken in this context, the existing voluntary industry codes of practice on environmental claims (or at least the ones we have seen) seem rather feeble. Voluntary codes may play their part in raising standards, and there is nothing to prevent retailers and industry from adopting their own codes now, but we cannot see how they could be made to work on a wider scale without statutory backing.

9. Setting standards: other environmental labelling schemes

A number of products bought during our shopping survey carried the logos or symbols of various organisations to show that they approved of or endorsed the product in some way and appeared to be connected to some sort of environmental claim. The schemes we came across were broadly of three types:

- licensing agreements, where the manufacturer has paid a fee to another organisation to use its logo and/or to gain their approval of the product carrying the logo;

- private approval and product endorsement schemes, where approval is granted by a separate organisation, usually on payment of a fee after certain standards have been met; and

- official approval schemes which have statutory backing or are backed by a national or international standards-making body.

The distinction between these categories is by no means clear-cut and is not obvious from the labelling and symbols used. We look at these three types of scheme at the start of this chapter and then at national and international systems of standards, eco-labelling and energy labelling.

Licensing agreements

Formal product licensing agreements arise when a company with a valuable trade mark, corporate logo or name allows a manufacturer or retailer to place it on its products in return for a fee. Such arrangements are normally agreed for a fixed period and certain conditions are attached. However, these may not always be made clear to or be known by the person buying the product.

Several products in our survey carried the World Wildlife Fund panda logo. When shown 55 environmental logos, most of the people in all the group discussions on environmental claims recognised this one. As one woman in the south commented, 'We know the panda, we've seen him for years'. On two of the products in our shopping survey, Ariel Future and Ronseal, the panda logo appeared next to and, certainly in the case of Ariel Future, could be considered part of, an environmental claim.

The World Wildlife Fund (WWF) did not respond formally to our consultation on environmental claims, but later provided helpful information about their activities. They say their panda logo, which their market research shows has an 84 per cent (prompted) awareness among the general public, is not to be regarded necessarily as a product endorsement, but as a licensing tool and a way of fund raising. In the past, the licensing of the logo has been used purely as a means of fund raising.

However, WWF is now developing environmental criteria - that is, certain hurdles which companies who apply to use the panda logo must get over - and a commitment to work with WWF to raise standards. The Ronseal Woodcare range is an example of a new type of partnership with WWF. The use of the logo by Procter & Gamble (on Ariel Future) is a strictly commercial deal. Under the terms of this latter deal, for which WWF is receiving a considerable donation, the company was permitted to put the panda symbol on Pampers disposable nappies, not a product which a full life-cycle analysis would normally certify as carrying positive environmental benefits. However, the symbol is not in fact used on this product. In a contract like this, a company such as Procter & Gamble is buying exclusivity in the marketplace. One of the terms of its licence is that no competing products can be offered the same rights to use the panda logo.

An article on corporate sponsorship in the autumn 1995 issue of *WWF News* encapsulates the current ambiguities in the licensed uses of the panda logo: 'With so many different types of corporate partnership, what does it mean when you see the panda logo alongside a corporate name? It means that WWF is receiving support from a company in terms of financial contributions, and probably benefiting from increased awareness of WWF's mission ... the panda logo is not an eco-label or endorsement, either of a product or a company's environmental status. WWF is very careful about who is allowed to use the logo and how it is used. Copyright laws protect the logo and stipulate how and when it may be reproduced. And this year, the Charities Act was amended so that in future, it should always be clear to the consumer why a charity logo is displayed in relation to a product, service or company name. It should also say how much money is being donated.' It would appear from the products we looked at that this had yet to be put into effect.

Approval schemes and product endorsements

Licensing of the panda logo may be moving in the direction of a private approval scheme. There is a surprisingly large number of these, although particular types of products seem to attract these schemes. The ones we found were mainly on products where there was a high level of consumer interest and concern about the environmental attributes of the product, such as with the production of food and concern about tropical rain forests. It is worth noting, too, that environmental claims about farming methods and the sources of timber are usually not verifiable by product testing or chemical analysis, so the consumer relies on the word of the producer.

... than conventional ... *Which?* its standards are not as strict as for ... to organic standards ['Food endorsement', *Which?* October 1995]. In addition, this is more of a product endorsement scheme than a conventional approvals scheme, given that the Guild will not endorse competing products, even if its standards are met. This is not made clear on the product label (for the full wording on the Jordan's Porridge Oats label see appendix 1, p. 135).

There is a bewildering number of approval schemes for timber and wood products. One that particularly impressed people in our group discussions was the claim on some teak garden furniture that it had been awarded in 1989 the Friends of the Earth 'Good Wood Seal of Approval' though no logo appears on the product. The brochure for these products goes on to say that, 'Many other hardwood timber products are currently marketed as sources from "sustained yield" forests, but to date these claims have not been recognised as substantiated by environmental agencies independent of the timber industry'.

Friends of the Earth (FoE) did not respond formally to our consultation on environmental claims, but later provided some helpful information. It says that the 'Good Wood Seal of Approval' scheme ran for only twelve months in 1989, and FoE did not expect its name to be used thereafter. Friends of the Earth product endorsements are, it insists, very rarely handed out and there have been none since 1989. It received no financial return for lending its name and, where it is still being used in this context, letters are sent to companies in an attempt to stop them using it. The organisation is also contemplating taking legal action.

Environmental groups have made a great effort in the last few years to try and establish an international certification or approval scheme for forest products.

In purs...
monitoring claims...
manufacturers, and in some...
made or the labelling is changed, the ...
a member of WWF asking for further details; th...
further letters which seek to persuade the supplier concern...
his claims [Mike Read Associates, letter to the NCC, 18 August 19...]

WWF has also established the 1995 group, a partnership with over forty UK companies. Members of this group are committed to phasing out wood and wood products which do not come from well managed forests verified as such by independent accredited certification schemes, by 31 December 1995. They are also committed to removing all other environmental claims and labels.

B&Q, the do-it-yourself products retailer, is a member of the 1995 group. Although it operates its own system of scrutiny of its wood suppliers, it strongly supports the concept of independent certification. The company thinks that 'for certification to have any value in the marketplace, certified products must bear a logo or a label ... which can be applied to any product, regardless of the certifier, country of origin or type of forest' [B&Q, *How Green is Your Front Door?* 1995]. The efforts of WWF and the 1995 group are aimed at clearing the timber and paper market of products making environmental claims and logos in order to pave the way for a new system of timber certification.

The Forest Stewardship Council (FSC) is an association founded in 1993 by a diverse group of representatives from environmental and social groups, the timber trade and the forestry profession. Based in Mexico, the FSC, which has its own logo (see the timber logos, appendix 4), will accredit and monitor organisations which certify forest and timber production. In other words, it will certify the certifiers [*FSC Notes*, summer 1995, volume 1, issue 1]. The FSC is currently evaluating four certifiers of which two, SGS Forestry and the Soil Association, are based in the UK. The 1995 group of retailers is committed to phasing in FSC-certified products as they become available. The ultimate aim of the FSC is to 'promote forest conservation through a market-driven selection of credibly-certified, sustainably-produced timber' [WWF, *Truth or Trickery? Timber Labelling Past, Present and Future*, March 1994].

The Soil Association launched its certificate of responsible forestry in 1993 with its own Woodmark (see timber logos, appendix 4) for timber products made from wood from forests meeting strictly defined environmental, social and economic criteria [*Living Earth and the Food Magazine*, November 1992]. The first forest to be certified is the Pengelli forest in Dyfed, and a chair made from wood from that forest is now on sale with the Woodmark symbol [*Living Earth and the Food Magazine*, April-June 1995].

There are several other timber certification schemes, or products bearing tree logos which could be interpreted as such. In the course of our shopping survey we came across a tree logo sponsored by a group of British traditional furniture makers called Woodland Heritage. Their aim is 'to improve the way in which trees (particularly broadleaf) are grown, maintained and harvested in these islands'. We also found the Woodland Trust logo on a piece of literature used to promote a paper recycling organisation. This logo was recognised by most of the people in our groups in the south, though not in the north. The Woodland Trust does not endorse any products, but it does enter into contractual sponsorship agreements whereby the company using its logo has to say that it is supporting its tree-planting programme or some other aspect of the Trust's work. In future it may endorse products using wood from its own woodlands.

While these and other labels fight to establish themselves in the marketplace, the problem for the consumer is to try and make an informed judgement about their varied claims.

Voluntary certification may extend to other products. Though not included in our shopping survey, the sources of plants and especially bulbs are coming under the scrutiny of environmental organisations. Fauna and Flora International (FFI) has been concerned for some time with the loss of wild plant species to the garden trade. They have had some success in promoting a labelling scheme for bulbs. The Dutch Bulb Exporters Association (DBEA), which consists of virtually all the Dutch bulb trade, has signed a labelling agreement with FFI. Under this, bulbs should be labelled as either 'bulbs from wild source' or 'bulbs grown from cultivated stock'. This is a voluntary agreement but includes detailed definitions for what constitutes 'wild'.

After lengthy discussion, the UK Bulb Distributors Association has agreed to an identical arrangement. However, in the UK, there are major bulb dealers who do not belong to the BDA, and Fauna and Flora International is negotiating with them individually. FFI publishes an annual *Good Bulb Guide*. This has two lists of companies. List A is those who 'never knowingly sell wild-collected bulbs' and list B those who make it clear to customers when bulbs are from a wild source. FFI monitors compliance and has deleted one company from this year's guide for its failure to 'never knowingly sell wild-collected bulbs'.

Statutory-backed approval schemes

Our shopping survey revealed a number of terms used to describe food that has been produced in a 'traditional' fashion, although the description 'organic' is the only one subject to national and European Union regulation. As with claims about the sourcing of timber and plants, one of the problems with organic food is that it cannot be tested to prove that it has been grown in a certain way. Even when tests have been used, as in Warwickshire County Council's failed efforts to prosecute an organic flour producer under the Trade Descriptions Act (see chapter 8), these might not be accepted by the courts.

The EU regulation (2092/91) on organic food production and labelling came into effect in 1993. Food may not be labelled as organically produced unless it complies with the standards laid down in the regulation. The regulation was, however, applied on top of an existing system of certifying organic food in the UK. This is based on the UK Register of Organic Food Standards (UKROFS), an organic standards regulatory body which accredits the UK-approved organic certification bodies. As at 1 January 1995 there were six organic certification organisations, each with its own logo (see appendix 4) which is attached to approved products. The Soil Association's scheme is by far the largest and best known. Apart from the symbols from the UK schemes, imported organic products will carry foreign symbols or manufacturers' labels claiming organic status.

All growers and processors of organic food are subject to inspection by approved organisations at least once a year and so 'there is reason to believe that consumers are being adequately safe-guarded in the environmental area of organic food labelling' [Soil Association, letter to the NCC, 8 June 1995]. The use of the word 'organic' on a label should thus be sufficient guarantee that the product has been produced organically under an inspected and certified scheme.

However, it is possible to buy products labelled as 'organic' which do not bear the logo or label of one of the schemes, and which may not have been independently inspected. In such cases the producers are themselves responsible for complying with the EU organic food regulations and, as with any other labelling claim, it would be up to local trading standards officers to prosecute if they had evidence of false labelling [*Living Earth and the Food Magazine*, April-June 1995]. Quite how they would obtain such evidence is not clear.

Another potential problem is that the regulation allows the EU countries to use different terms to mean organic in the food context. In Spanish it is 'ecologico' (with a similar word in Danish, German and Greek); in French it is 'biologique' (with a similar word in Italian, Dutch and Portuguese). Only English has 'organic' [article 2 of the Council of Europe Regulation no. 2092/91].

Standards

Standards are a form of certification of products and services to show that they meet particular levels of performance. Accreditation is voluntary but, once granted, companies and organisations which produce the certified product or source can use this information in their promotional campaigns. Although standards do not have the force of law, non-adherence to the established UK or international standard can be cited in prosecutions and used by magistrates and judges in helping them to decide whether a trade description is false or misleading. Since one of the problems with environmental claims is the lack of certainty about their validity, the establishment of clear standards could go some way towards adding certainty. Even if comparatively few companies were to go through the hassle and expense of applying for approval under a standard, many more might adopt them unofficially and they could be used as a clear benchmark for what is acceptable or unacceptable in environmental claims.

Currently, there are no British Standards on environmental claims. However, work is under way in the International Standards Organisation (ISO) on four relevant standards. Once the ISO starts work on a subject, work by national standards-making bodies ceases, so the British Standards Institution (BSI) is no longer directly involved in this area although it does contribute to the ISO work. ISO technical committee number 207 on environmental management has produced four draft standards on environmental claims. These are:

- ISO 14020 on environmental labelling, which sets out the basic principles to be followed by all environmental labelling schemes;

- ISO 14021 on self-declaration environmental claims, which looks at manufacturers' and retailers' labels;

- ISO 14022 which deals with symbols and logos;

- and ISO 14023 on testing and verification methodologies.

So far, real progress has only been made on the first two standards, and there are substantial problems to be overcome before the final versions are agreed. There has probably never been an attempt to secure world-wide agreement on misleading claims of any kind before, and it is certainly a new area of work for an organisation that is used to dealing with very technical issues [John Lawrance, 'Environmental labelling and international standardisation', *ITSA Review*, summer 1995]. Since the process of agreeing standards proceeds by consensus and involves many different countries, it is extremely slow. International standards on environmental claims are still in prospect, but perhaps many years away.

Eco-labelling

Eco-labels are an officially-approved type of environmental label. In appearance, they are usually in the form of a logo which is attached to products that meet some prescribed environmental criteria and that have been independently tested and approved as meeting those criteria. Normally, the manufacturer applying for the eco-label pays a fee to use it and to have the product tested. Eco-labels generally give an overall assessment of a product's environmental quality relative to other products in its category. They are usually based on an analysis of the life-cycle of the product, encompassing its manufacture from raw materials, its distribution, use by the consumer and its eventual disposal.

Many countries now have their own eco-labelling schemes. The longest running is the German 'blue angel' scheme which issued its first label in 1978 and now covers nearly 4,000 products [OECD, *Environmental Labelling in OECD Countries*, Paris, 1991]. The schemes depend for their success on wide consumer recognition and acceptance of the label, to make it worth the expense to the producer of applying for one, and on the existence of objective criteria and consistent test methods to maintain the integrity of the label.

That the principle of eco-labelling is attractive to consumers seems to have been confirmed by people who took part in our market research. When discussing the issue of competing and confusing environmental labels and symbols, people in the discussion groups thought it would be a good idea if claims and symbols were standardised (see chapter 5). Some suggested that one standardised symbol should be used for each main aspect, such as 'recycled', ' CFC free' or 'conserving water', in the same way that different symbols make up the washing instructions on clothes labels. Others, however, seemed to prefer the idea of one overall symbol that would be easily recognised.

Their suggestions included: 'If you saw something like that - a green spot on everything - and it incorporated all these statements that they're making, you could pick up the packet, "it's got the green spot, I'll buy it"'. And, 'It would be easier if there was one symbol that everyone recognised like a British Kitemark - that everybody could look at and think, "oh, ok, that's fine"'. Another said: 'And you assume it's tested by an independent body to maintain that standard'. And 'What you need is a symbol that no matter where you are in the world (it's the same)'.

These suggestions are matched fairly closely by the European Union's own eco-labelling scheme. This is administered in this country by the UK Eco-Labelling Board. Our shoppers found the eco-label on one product, the Hoover New Wave washing machine. As yet, it appears only on that product. The scheme has been very slow to get under way. Hoover claims that the result of gaining the eco-label was to treble its market share in Germany and to double its market in the premium sector of the UK automatic washing machine market [Mike Rutter, Hoover marketing director, quoted by UK Eco-labelling Board, 1995].

The EU eco-label

Perhaps it is still early days for the eco-label, but no one in our groups of shoppers recognised the logo, though some guessed it had something to do with the European Union. Others commented that it was too 'pretty' to have any official status. Currently, the eco-label has to fight for recognition from consumers against a plethora of unofficial designs and logos. There is nothing on it to indicate that it has any special status.

In the very long term, the existence of a credible, independently certified and tested eco-label, applied to a wide range of products, could provide valuable help to consumers in guiding them through the maze of conflicting environmental information. But we cannot be optimistic that the scheme will become well established in the face of reluctance from manufacturers to apply for eco-labels. Indeed, currently, there seems little incentive for them to go to the bother and expense of doing so, when they can freely apply their own environmental symbols and claims to products, and consumers are unable to distinguish between these and the genuine article.

Energy labelling

Another type of environmental label which is beginning to appear on appliances is the energy label. Energy labels give ratings for appliances based on their consumption of energy under standard conditions. Under EU legislation which came into effect in January 1994, it is compulsory to label domestic appliances with information about how much energy they use.

The design of the label and type of information it can carry are fixed in the legislation (see the box on the next page), and the regulations have been applied to successive types of appliance. Since January 1995 all new fridges and freezers have had to carry labels, and the regulations for washing machines and tumble-dryers will apply from April 1996. Other appliances will follow later.

What the new energy label says

(1) The energy efficiency class shows at a glance how efficient each model is compared with others on the market in the same product group. An 'A' represents the most efficient and 'G' is the worst. An efficiency class of 'D' applies to those products that have an average energy efficiency. The average energy consumption is based upon the product class for those appliances which were on the market in 1992.

(2) The 'Ecolabel' is shown on the energy label for those appliances which have qualified for this award.

(3) The label shows the energy use of the appliance in kilowatt hours (kWh) each year. This can be converted to an annual cost by multiplying by the tariff rate.

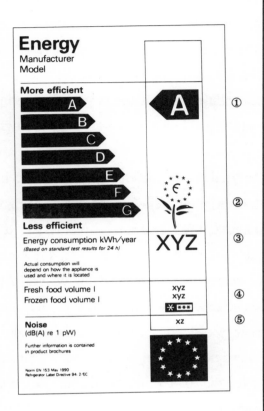

(4) The capacity of the fridge freezer compartments is shown in litres. The star rating which refers to the coldest compartment is as follows:

* colder than or equal to - 6°C
** colder than or equal to - 12°C
*** colder than or equal to - 18°C
**** also maintains a temperature of - 18°C and has the ability to freeze products quickly.

(5) Noise - this will be important to some people. There is a technical test to comply with the European Union regulations on noise emissions from household appliances. Data is currently not available and it is unlikely to be in force in the UK in the near future.

(source: 'Hydro-Know How', Scottish Hydro Electric)

The theory behind energy labelling is that since a quarter of all the electricity used in the UK is used for domestic lighting and appliances, if consumers could work out how much electricity their appliances consumed, they might in future choose those that use the least. The government's strategy for climate change recognises this, and the energy labelling of appliances is expected to contribute towards the target of lowering UK emissions of carbon dioxide (which adds to global warming) through reduced consumption of electricity.

An analysis of the energy used in the lifecycle of fridges and freezers shows that three-quarters is used during their working life, rather than during their manufacture, transport to retailers or disposal. This is also true for most major domestic appliances, as, for instance, in washing machines where a lot of energy is used to heat the water. Although new appliances generally use less energy now than earlier models, there is still a great variation in the energy efficiency of appliances on sale. For identical levels of service, the electricity consumption of the most inefficient new appliance is more than twice that of the most efficient one, and this applies to cookers, fridge-freezers, washing machines, tumble-dryers, and dishwashers [see Environmental Change Unit, *DECADE: second year report*, Oxford, 1995, our source for most of this section].

At the time of our shopping survey, only fridges, freezers and fridge-freezers had to carry the EU-approved energy label, and these were noted by our shoppers (see appendix 1). As it happened, no one in our groups of shoppers who took part in the market research had bought one of these appliances in the previous four months, so it is not surprising that no one had noticed the label or commented on the scheme. They were not shown pictures of the label during the discussions. People in our groups talked about the factors that were important to them when choosing a fridge, freezer or fridge-freezer. They mentioned the brand, reliability, cubic capacity and use of space as key issues, and some also talked about electricity consumption and running costs.

For washing machines, choosing and sticking with a reliable brand was the main factor in selecting a machine, along with price. Beyond this, manufacturers' claims about saving water (important for those on water meters) and saving electricity were mentioned as factors affecting choice in some cases, and a few also talked about other aspects such as the number and type of programmes and spin speeds.

As energy labels are a recent innovation, it is rather early to judge whether they will be successful, as the government hopes, in guiding people to choose the more energy efficient 'A' and 'B'-rated appliances in preference to those rated 'F' and 'G'. There are some pointers to their likely success.

Consumers' Association, publishers of *Which?* magazine, have tested and rated appliances for their energy consumption for many years, and include this information in their magazine reports. Energy efficiency is one of the factors they take into account in recommending their 'best buys'. Judging by their February 1995 report on fridges and freezers, however, low running costs would not outweigh other factors in assessing the performance of a fridge or freezer, though they are an important consideration. *Which?* weight their test results, when making recommendations, to give greater emphasis to the technical aspects of the product which they consider to be the most important. For fridges the main weights are temperature range 25 per cent, temperature stability 25 per cent, energy efficiency 20 per cent, de-frosting 7.5 per cent [*Which?* February 1995]. As a result of these weights, some of the recommended 'best buys' for fridges in February 1995 did not score as highly for energy efficiency as some models which were not recommended, though they outperformed them on these other aspects.

It is very early days for the energy label, and there is little information on whether consumers actually use and understand the label, let alone whether it influences their choice. The DECADE team conducted a pilot survey in the summer of 1995 with a sample of 220 people in the Oxford area who had bought a fridge since the introduction of the scheme in January. Over a third of those who responded said that the fridge they bought had an energy label (37 per cent), but 16 per cent said there was no label, and nearly half (47 per cent) did not know. Over half of those who had noticed the label (58 per cent) said that they found the label easy to understand, though many would have liked more information. Only 15 per cent said that the label had influenced their purchase 'a great deal', though a further 19 per cent said it had influenced them 'quite a lot'. In choosing a new fridge the most important considerations for people in this survey were:

Cost	35%
How well it would work	20%
Energy efficiency or 'environmental friendliness'	15%
Place of manufacture	15%
Features	5%
Expected life span	4%
Size	4%
Appearance	2%

A key factor identified in this survey was the importance of sales staff in giving advice and information. About half of the fridge buyers mentioned them as an important source of information. This supports other research into consumer buying behaviour which suggests that consumers get much of their information when deciding on major purchases such as appliances from retail staff [see M. R. Solomon, *Consumer Behaviour*, 3rd edition, Prentice Hall, 1995].

The problem from the point of view of anyone wishing to promote energy efficiency through consumers modifying their buying patterns is that the retail sector tends to be dominated by purchase price considerations. Manufacturers of electrical appliances are under no pressure to provide energy-efficient appliances to appliance showrooms. As the director of the Association of Manufacturers of Domestic Electrical Appliances put it to a recent conference: 'Manufacturers and the energy conservationists are - in this retail sector - frustrated in their efforts to encourage consumers to buy quality, innovation and energy efficiency by a ferocious price war in what we used to call the High Street' [Peter Carver, speech to conference at St Hilda's College Oxford organised by DECADE, 7 December 1995].

One retailer which has given greater emphasis to energy efficiency in appliances is Scottish Hydro-Electric, which has 55 shops mainly in the north of Scotland. Scottish Hydro-Electric (SHE) launched the energy label for refrigeration equipment in June 1994, six months ahead of the rest of Europe. In order to do this, they had to assess the ratings and label all the stock themselves, as well as train staff and produce factsheets for customers and staff. The main effort was put into the development of a new training module for staff to enable them to explain the information on the label to customers. According to the company, sales of the most energy-efficient appliances rose markedly in the first four to six weeks after the label was launched, and have been sustained since then. As a result, while in March 1994 only 38 per cent of the fridges held in stock were of average efficiency or above (rated 'A' to 'D') by February 1995 this had risen to 85 per cent. The company has since followed up its initiative on refrigeration by introducing energy-labelled tumble-driers, ahead of the EU deadline, and will launch energy labels for washing-machines, washer-dryers and dishwashers in 1996 [presentation by David Simpson, Business Support Manager, Scottish Hydro-Electric to DECADE conference, Oxford, 7 December 1995].

The Scottish Hydro-Electric experiment appears to be unique among UK retailers at present. One factor in their success may be the low density of population (their 55 shops cover a quarter of the UK landmass), which means that buyers of appliances are unlikely to visit many competing outlets because of the vast travel distances involved. In more densely populated areas, where competing retailers are virtually next door to each other, price does seem to be the key factor, with other messages drowned out. Another problem for the energy label in gaining consumer confidence is that the reliability of some of the information on it is open to question. Consumers' Association has criticised it because the electricity consumption figures on it are not verified independently. They are supplied by the manufacturers of the appliances. In tests reported in February 1995, of thirty-two fridges and freezers tested, nearly half (15) used at least 15 per cent more energy than the manufacturers claimed [*Which?* February 1995].

Energy labelling is a limited form of environmental labelling as it does not deal with other factors connected with the environmental impact of products. The new EU energy label is compulsory for the products to which it is applied but there seems to have been no publicity about the introduction of the label, and little research, prior to its introduction, into whether people will understand it and use it. Currently, energy efficiency is a consideration when people are choosing electrical appliances, but not the prime deciding factor. It is possible that retailers will help educate consumers into the benefits of buying the most energy-efficient appliances. This currently looks unlikely in a marketplace which is generally dominated by discounters who can see no incentive for investing in staff training and consumer education about the intricacies of the energy label. As with the other labelling schemes discussed in this chapter, there is nothing obvious to consumers about the energy label to suggest that it is particularly different from other schemes, other than that it appears on all appliances. It is difficult to assess how much credence consumers will give it in the longer term in the absence of significant retailing and advertising support.

Conclusion

Product endorsement, certification, eco-labelling and voluntary labelling schemes - and perhaps international standards one day - may all play their part in defining the types of environmental claims that are being made. But the existence of so many schemes, usually with the attendant paraphernalia of certificates, symbols on products and complicated explanations and labels, creates a bewildering maze of information, much of it contradictory, which has to be assessed by consumers. It is little wonder, then, that the reaction of consumers in our ordinary shopper groups was to give up the struggle to make sense of them all and the reaction of our group of light green consumers was to press on, more in hope than expectation that their purchasing decisions were going to have any positive effect. Consumers are in no position to judge the relative merits of any of these competing schemes. The evidence from our opinion research among shoppers seems to be that they do respect the endorsement of well-known independent bodies like the WWF and Friends of the Earth. However, our research has also shown that products with the endorsement of these organisations are not necessarily offering any greater environmental benefits than those without them.

10. Environmental claims in other countries

The use of environmental claims in marketing is a world-wide phenomenon. Many countries now have government-sponsored environmental labelling schemes which seek to establish some sort of standard for environmental improvements in various products, together with an accreditation scheme for products which reach those standards. This is usually communicated to consumers in some form of label and wording on the product. Many countries have also legislated, or taken other action, against false or misleading environmental claims on products or in advertising. The National Consumer Council has not been able to look at all of these in detail, but we have examined the interesting approaches adopted in Sweden, a fellow member of the European Union, in the USA, where many green marketing claims originally came from, and in Australia.

Sweden

Before joining the European Union, Sweden had already developed its own comprehensive regulations on the control of misleading product descriptions, through its Consumer Ombudsman and Market Court. In this system, marketing and advertising claims are dealt with in the same way. When Sweden joined the European Union and implemented EU law, there was no need to change the way advertising and marketing claims were dealt with since the EU directive on the control of misleading advertising defines advertising in such a way as to encompass claims on products. So, in Sweden, marketing claims must be capable of being substantiated in exactly the same way as advertising, and this includes environmental claims. Since the Swedish treatment of claims is in accordance with the EU directive, it cannot constitute a trade barrier.

The Market Court has found against several companies using the word 'Miljö' (which means 'environment') in their product name, on the grounds that they gave the impression the product was environmentally friendly when what amounted to an analysis of the product's life cycle showed that it could not possibly substantiate this. So in 1974 the use of the word in the product name of a degreaser, Exynol Miljö, was found misleading after it was shown it could poison fish when discharged into water courses. In 1990 the use of the word in marketing a domestic heating oil was also prohibited. The company claimed the oil Hydro Miljö Plus produced less soot and was more efficient than other heating oils, but it was not permitted, in the court decision, to use the word in its product name or to describe itself as 'the environmentally friendly oil' because the court considered that the company had failed to show that it differed significantly from other boiler oils [National Swedish Board for Consumer Policies, *Environmental Arguments in Marketing*, May 1995].

The United States

In the United States (and Australia - see below), controls on the use of environmental claims are applied under the legal umbrella of general consumer legislation prohibiting deceptive trade practices. In the USA this is contained in the Federal Trade Commission Act. Section 5 of this Act makes deceptive acts and practices in or affecting commerce unlawful. The Federal Trade Commission (FTC) is charged with enforcement. It is empowered to make rules and to issue guides, and guidance forms an important part of its activities.

As at 1993, the FTC had 35 rules in operation and 37 guides. The guides indicate how advertisers and marketers can conform with legal requirements. 'Conduct inconsistent with the positions articulated in these guides may result in corrective action by the Commission under section 5 if, after investigation, the Commission has reason to believe that the behaviour falls within the scope of conduct declared unlawful by the statute' [*Federal Register* vol. 57, 13 August 1992]. Prior to issuing guidelines on environmental claims, the FTC had brought eight actions against companies making allegedly misleading environmental claims in two years.

The FTC's *Guidelines for the Use of Environmental Marketing Claims* were introduced in 1992 after extensive consultation and two days of national hearings. They are currently being reviewed. At present, they are very wide-ranging and apply to advertising, labelling and other forms of marketing to consumers, and include logos, symbols, product brand names, promotional materials and claims asserted directly or by implication.

Anyone making an express or implied claim is required to be able to substantiate it, using competent and reliable evidence which may well be scientific evidence. The FTC will find that there has been deception 'if there is a representation, omission or practice that is likely to mislead the consumer acting reasonably in the circumstances, to the consumer's detriment [FTC policy statement on deception, quoted in the *Federal Register*, vol. 57, 13 August 1992]. The guidelines lay down four general principles to be followed in making environmental claims, and give specific guidance on eight common claims with examples of good and bad practice.

General claims about a product's benefit to the environment must be avoided or qualified, unless every particular can be substantiated - which effectively gets rid of most of these claims. Claims about degradability can only be used if they can be substantiated to show that the product will 'decompose into elements found in nature within a reasonably short period of time'. Again, this would exclude most claims unless they were heavily qualified. Other specific guidance is given on 'compostable', ' recyclable', ' recycled content', claims about using reduced resources, 'refillable,' and 'ozone-safe' and 'ozone-friendly'.

Since the guidelines were issued, the FTC has stepped up its law enforcement activity. It has pursued seven cases on degradability claims on disposable nappies and rubbish bags. These were comparative claims which the companies were unable to substantiate, mainly because most of this waste is landfilled and the aim of landfill management is to slow down degradation. There have also been seven cases on 'CFC-free' and 'environmentally friendly' aerosols which contained other ozone-depleting substances, such as HCFCs. Cases are usually resolved by negotiation [paper given by Deborah K. Owen, Commissioner, Federal Trade Commission, to the Florida Bar Business Law Seminar, Miami, 14 September 1993, available on the US government site on the Internet]. Although the guidelines are now being reviewed, this is part of a regular process by which they are kept up to date. According to the USA consumer organisation, Consumers Union, they are working well [personal communication to NCC].

Australia

The Australian Trade Practices Commission (TPC) is similar in some respects to the US Federal Trade Commission. The Trade Practices Act, and similar legislation at state level, prohibit misleading or deceptive conduct and certain false or misleading representations. Consumer affairs authorities in the states or the Commission itself can take action in the courts to restrain conduct or to insist on corrective advertising. Competitors and others can sue for compensation for their losses if breach of the law is established.

The TPC's *Environmental Guidelines* are designed to promote compliance with the general legislation, and to encourage industry to regulate itself by developing codes of practice for advertising and promotion. The guidelines define what is misleading or deceptive conduct within the terms of the Act, and give examples. The test is objective - is the claim likely to mislead or deceive? It can be explicit, by implication or contextual. Silence or a partial truth can also be deceptive. If the claim is factual, the Act will be breached unless it is capable of substantiation. Environmental benefits should be spelt out, but the claim must use language the average member of the public can understand, and it must be able to be substantiated. Unqualified statements such as 'environmentally friendly' or 'safe' should be avoided, as should 'green' and the environmental benefits must be real and relevant.

The guidelines also offer guidance on the use of terms commonly found in environmental claims such as 'recycled' and 'biodegradable' but they are not as prescriptive as the US guidelines. They also provide a useful eight point checklist for marketers to evaluate claims before they are used. They include a section on product endorsement schemes.

Since publishing the guidelines, the TPC has been involved in a number of enforcement actions covering a wide range of products, from toilet paper to batteries for mobile telephones. The guidelines are now under review, especially with regard to their possible effects on trade. The aim is to keep regulations in step with Australia's main trading partners [Trade Practices Commission, *Fair Trading*, Canberra, July 1995].

11. Tackling misleading green claims: the options

Our research demonstrates that there is a substantial problem with confusing and misleading environmental claims. This mainly takes the form of dubious claims on products and their packaging. Although only a minority of consumers actually look out for these claims when shopping, all, including those who claim to be more environmentally aware, find the claims confusing and have been misled by them. The legal remedies for dealing with environmental product claims are too cumbersome. They invoke the full panoply of the criminal law, with its high standards of proof, to deal with claims, some of which are too vague and non-specific to be caught by legislation of this type and others of which are defined so tightly that they also evade the law. As it stands, the law does not effectively regulate environmental product claims and is no deterrent.

If the UK is to meet its environmental policy goals, it needs the confidence and co-operation of informed consumers, who have the potential to transform markets by demanding, and receiving, less environmentally harmful products from manufacturers. If they are being bombarded by confusing and misleading environmental claims on products, consumers are unlikely to be able to play their part.

Any claim has to be tested in the light of its impact on consumers. There is a need for clear, simple, truthful and authoritative statements about the environmental impact of products. The statements must be both coherent and consistent. They should be written in language likely to be understood by ordinary people and be capable of substantiation, to a reasonably objective standard, by the person making the claim. The regulation of claims needs to be flexible, so that it can incorporate future scientific and technical developments and be updated readily. Enforcement measures need to be simple, clear to consumers, effective, and achievable at reasonable cost, both to those enforcing any regulations and to those complying with them. They should not introduce barriers to trade.

In the rest of this chapter, we look at the pros and cons of four possible measures for tackling misleading claims.

Option 1: amend the Trade Descriptions Act 1968

Our report has discussed the Trade Descriptions Act extensively. The Act already covers product claims, if imperfectly, and has an established method of enforcement through local authorities' trading standards departments which have developed considerable expertise in the field. The strength of the Trade Descriptions Act lies in the fact that it provides a criminal sanction against those who make false and misleading statements about products. It therefore already catches the worst sort of claims. And it could scarcely be argued that it constitutes any sort of barrier to trade.

We have already suggested (in chapter 8) that a minor amendment to section 2 would ensure that the Act would cover at least those statements about the environmental impact of products that fall within the definition of 'false' or 'misleading'. However, it might be possible to go further, to catch hyperbolic environmental statements like 'ozone friendly' which, though probably false, are not 'false to a material degree' as currently required by the Act. A new section could be added which would say that, in respect of claims as to the environmental impact of products, a statement would be false to a material degree if it had no factual basis. A statement which used hyperbolic language, such as 'ozone friendly' could then be defined as having no factual basis unless the product was better than the average standard for products in its class. One positive effect of this would be that products that were genuinely better than average would have no problems making environmental claims.

Amending the Trade Descriptions Act in this way would give trading standards officers extra grounds to bring prosecutions and extra confidence to bring them. It might also prompt manufacturers and retailers to moderate their environmental claims if there was a greater likelihood of being successfully prosecuted.

The main disadvantage of adapting the existing legislation in this way is that the definition of a false or misleading statement would never cover the sort of statement which might be true but is impossible to prove or to verify. Unfortunately, as our investigation of the current marketing claims shows, there are very many environmental claims where there is no accepted definition, where the scientific evidence is ambiguous, or where the claim can only be proved or disproved at disproportionate cost. Trading standards officers and others lack access to the detailed knowledge which could help them establish the accuracy or otherwise of many environmental claims. This seems to us to be a large obstacle to making enforcement effective, even under an amended Act, unless the Act were to be further amended to criminalise the making of unsubstantiated claims. We do not believe that this would be acceptable in the context of the Trade Descriptions Act.

Option 2: introduce an Environmental Claims Act

The introduction of specific legislation to deal with environmental claims, though costly in parliamentary time, would have several advantages over a straightforward amendment of the Trade Descriptions Act. A self-contained measure would raise the profile of legislation on environmental claims and encourage greater voluntary compliance with its provisions. It would also be possible to introduce a requirement that those making environmental claims should be in a position to substantiate them, without imposing this requirement on people making other sorts of marketing claim.

The Environmental Claims Bill, a private member's bill which failed in 1994, is the only proposal at present in this area. The Bill covers animal welfare as well as environmental claims. Although it is a stand-alone measure and does not seek to amend the Trade Descriptions Act, it adopts the wording of part of that Act in its definition of 'false and misleading'. The Bill also makes it a criminal offence to make an unsupported claim and covers claims made in advertisements. It would give the Secretary of State power to ascribe definite meanings to words, symbols and expressions used in claims, and to prohibit their use in claims. The Secretary of State could publish a code of practice under this Bill on the use of claims. If the company making the claim could show that it adhered to a code of practice, this would be accepted by the court as a defence in the event of prosecution.

The Bill covers the claimed impact of goods and services on the environment, false claims, misleading claims that verge on hyperbole, and statements which, though in themselves true, fail to mention relevant facts which would put a very different complexion on the statement. The combined effects of sections 1 and part 4 of section 3 together would make it an offence to make an unsupported claim, which is defined as a claim 'made without belief' in its truth. This goes a great deal further than simply to cover statements which are false or misleading. The trader would be liable if there were no reasonable grounds for making the claim. Section 9 requires the trader to keep a record, if he is aware of any information supporting his claim, and to produce it if requested to do so by a trading standards officer. So it reverses the burden of proof.

The Environmental Claims Bill has been opposed on a number of different grounds and chief among these is the reversal of the burden of proof (the requirement to substantiate claims). This is unusual in the criminal law, but not unheard of in other consumer legislation where normal means of enforcement by testing or sampling is impossible.

For example, in the legislation on average quantity under the Weights and Measures Act 1985, manufacturers are required to hold documentation on their sampling and testing to ensure that, during a production run, the prescribed average quantities are being achieved. Several pieces of consumer protection legislation derived from EU directives also require manufacturers to keep records and information available for inspection by the authorities. For example, this applies to the toy safety regulations and to the new regulations on the labelling of cosmetics ingredients, which are to be implemented under the Consumer Protection Act in 1996. These last regulations require manufacturers and those responsible for placing cosmetics on the market to keep detailed information on the identity, amounts, suppliers and safety of the ingredients used and proof of the effect claimed for each cosmetic ingredient and product [DTI, Cosmetic Product Directive 76/768/EEC, sixth amendment 93/35/EEC draft statutory instrument, October 1995]. The information must be kept 'readily accessible' to the enforcement authorities.

On the face of it, the requirement to keep a record substantiating any environmental claims could constitute a barrier to trade, and so infringe article 30 of the Treaty of Rome. It would impede the free movement of goods, by making life difficult for importers who would have to provide documentary evidence to substantiate environmental claims on their products. The question is whether this requirement could be justified as a measure of consumer protection.

There have been a reasonable number of cases on this in the European Court of Justice, where arguments that protectionist measures whose effect is to restrict imports are really to protect consumers have been struck down (including a famous case [Rau 261/81] where margarine had to be repackaged in cubes to 'protect consumers'). However, the requirement simply to keep certain records 'if [the trader] is aware of any information in support of the claim' is not nearly so prescriptive, nor does it have such an impact on a company's marketing strategy or profitability.

In practice, the European Court has not struck down other legislation when it has been persuaded of a compelling need to protect consumers. It is at least arguable that an encouragement to keep records, and therefore to be more responsible about claims which may influence environmentally-concerned consumers, is an important consumer protection aim and therefore no barrier to trade, particularly where it can be shown that environmental claims are difficult to prove and that substantiation of claims is required in other European Union countries.

The requirement to keep records could be a significant improvement in terms of enforcing the law on misleading environmental claims. As we have seen, some other pieces of consumer legislation already require manufacturers to keep records in order to assist law enforcement, so it is not such a novel idea. Furthermore, all advertisers, under the terms of the advertising codes, have to be able to substantiate claims. Most responsible manufacturers do not in any case make product claims without evidence to support them. The legal requirement to keep records might simply serve to remind them to do this more systematically. Some would, however, argue that there would be some compliance costs, though realistically we believe them to be modest.

The Local Authorities Co-ordinating Body on Food and Trading Standards (LACOTS) has criticised the Environmental Claims Bill on the grounds that it will not tackle the problems it has identified. It is not opposed to clarifying the legislation, to make it clear that environmental claims are a trade description, but it does not believe this is the root of the problem. In LACOTS' view, the record-keeping provision could be easily circumvented, because it only relates to information voluntarily retained. So the problem of gathering evidence would remain as difficult as before.

As it stands, the Bill suffers from poor drafting and a tendency to mirror provisions, such as the power to make definition orders, already contained in the Trade Descriptions Act but which have never been used. The keeping of records clause could possibly be amended to make it more effective, and there might be scope for including a statutory framework for codes of practice, to be drawn up in consultation with industry, consumer and environmental experts, which would give detailed guidance on the acceptability of certain types of claim in particular industries.

Option 3: extend the scope of the Advertising Standards Authority

The Advertising Standards Authority already deals with misleading environmental claims made in most forms of advertisement other than on the product itself and in broadcasting. Under the advertising codes of practice it administers, the advertiser must be able to substantiate claims if challenged. Certain types of environmental claim, such as the ubiquitous 'environmentally friendly' may not be used unless the advertiser can show from an analysis of the product's life cycle that it is true in comparison with other products in its class.

This regulation is voluntary, is paid for by the advertising industry itself (though the cost is presumably eventually recouped through the higher cost of heavily advertised products), is accessible to consumers, well-known and well-established. In the field of environmental claims, it seems currently to be working reasonably well, due in part to the development of improved codes on advertised environmental claims. It provides for a 'softer' system of regulatory enforcement than the full panoply of the criminal law, though it is backed up by civil law remedies when necessary. Why not simply extend the ASA's brief to cover product claims as well?

In Sweden there is no distinction between advertising and on-product claims, and the Swedish system for adjudicating claims comes under the same EU directive on misleading advertising as the UK system. The definition of advertising in the directive is very broad and has been adopted as a straight translation into both UK and Swedish law. It states that 'in these Regulations "advertisement" means any form of representation which is made in connection with a trade, business, craft or profession in order to promote the supply or transfer of goods or services, immovable property, rights or obligations'. 'Any form of representation made in connection with a trade' clearly includes product claims, and it is possible to argue that the current UK system of advertising control implements only part of the directive. Indeed, Department of Trade and Industry lawyers have advised us that the UK system of self-regulation by the advertising industry could be extended to cover on-pack claims without any need for legislation.

From the point of view of dealing with environmental claims, extending the Advertising Standards Association's remit to cover claims on the pack, as well as all non-broadcast advertising, would make a lot of sense. All environmental claims could then be dealt with in a consistent and logical manner by one authority. The distinction between on-pack and advertising claims is in any case artificial. Packs are not designed in isolation. The product labelling, design, packaging and advertising are part of one marketing process. At present it is theoretically possible - and it does happen in practice - that claims that would not be allowed in advertising appear on the pack, and are simply alluded to in the advertisements by, for example, the use of 'green' imagery. The fundamental problem of having several different systems to control marketing and advertising claims is that, collectively, they are only as strong as the weakest link in the chain. Currently with environmental claims, that weak link is with on-pack claims. The only method of dealing with them is through enforcement of the Trade Descriptions Act which is not itself designed for the job. From the consumers' point of view, it makes little difference who deals with a misleading claim as long as it *is* dealt with and they can rely on the truthfulness of statements that are made about products.

Giving adjudication to the Advertising Standards Association over product claims might solve the disparities in treatment of environmental claims, but it would have implications for other (non-environmental) product claims, some of which are also causing the enforcement authorities and consumers problems - like animal welfare, and nutrition and health claims. The ASA has made it clear in discussions with us that, though ideally it might well be considered the logical body to deal with all marketing and advertising claims and it would be relatively simple to take on environmental claims, in practice it would have to take on all product claims.

The resource implications of this would be substantial, and it is not at all clear how it could be financed. As we have said, the ASA is financed by a voluntary levy, paid by advertisers. For every product label and claim forming part of a co-ordinated marketing strategy that includes advertising, there must be thousands of products for which the packaging and labelling is the only element of the marketing strategy. Why should advertisers pay a levy to fund the regulation of misleading claims made by non-advertisers? On the other hand, there is a precedent, in that the ASA took over responsibility for monitoring claims made in direct marketing, after a separate system for dealing with these had been established. The industry might well prefer to sort out its own self-regulatory system rather than deal with amended legislation.

We have considered, briefly, whether any other body could set up a system for dealing with environmental claims on products that might mirror, and perhaps work alongside, the Advertising Standards Association. Remote possibilities are the Packaging Standards Council, an industry body which co-ordinates the views of the packaging industry and its consumers, or INCPEN, the Industry Council for Packaging and the Environment, which deals with the technical and environmental issues connected with packaging. Finance would again be a problem. But if the packaging industry is to sort out some sort of levy system to deal with its recycling commitments, perhaps it could also consider financing a system for monitoring and adjudicating misleading environmental claims on products?

If the ASA, or some other body, took over the supervision of environmental claims on products, its functions would overlap with trading standards officers. This already happens to some extent, and trading standards departments regularly refer complaints to the ASA. It would be important that this could continue and that the ASA, or whichever organisation it was, could refer cases back to the relevant home authority where it appeared that a prosecution under the Trade Descriptions Act was both warranted and likely to succeed. One final advantage of bringing product claims within the advertising regulations is that there should be no adverse implications for trade. As the EU directive already covers marketing claims, extending the current system could be presented as complying with the letter of the directive. There would also be no need for new legislation.

Option 4: establish a code of practice within a statutory framework

Both the Australian and United States legal systems deal with misleading environmental claims under a series of codes or guidelines, issued under the umbrella of general legal prohibitions on deceptive trade practices. The very great merit of this system is that the codes or guidelines can be flexible and readily updated to deal with changes in marketing, a point of great importance in the context of environmental claims. As Sainsbury's pointed out in its response to our consultation letter: 'formation of very specific legislation is costly in terms of the government's time in initial development and then the inevitable subsequent updating. Encoding today's "best practice" could in later years inhibit the development of "environmentally friendly" products as technology moves on but the legislative requirements remain static' [J. Sainsbury, letter to the NCC, 31 July 1995]. The other great benefit of a code is that it could be broadly consensual and policed, to some extent, by the marketers making claims, just as the ASA codes are used by competitors complaining about their rivals' advertising. It also allows for less draconian enforcement than the full machinery of the criminal law, frequently via negotiation, while enforcing higher standards, such as the requirement to substantiate claims.

There is no current provision in English statute for a general legal prohibition on deceptive trade practices under which a code or guide on the use of environmental claims in marketing could be agreed. There is, however, a long-standing proposal from the Director General of Fair Trading to replace part III of the Fair Trading Act, which most agree is not working as it was originally intended. The proposal is for a broadly-worded piece of legislation which can be used to 'sweep up business malpractice which harms consumers and puts reputable businesses at a competitive disadvantage' [Office of Fair Trading, *Trading Malpractices: a report by the DGFT following consideration of proposals for a general duty to trade fairly*, July 1990, p. 3].

The current proposals to reform part III of the Act were issued for consultation at the beginning of 1995 and the National Consumer Council responded to them in April 1995 [NCC, *Reform of Part III of the Fair Trading Act*, 1995]. We support the key elements of the latest proposals, though we think that the enforcement and the sanctions suggested in the current consultation should be amended. As they stand, the proposals would concentrate on tackling unlawful, deceptive or objectionable business practices which other legislation cannot control effectively. They would extend the definition of 'unfair' to include deceptive or misleading, with an illustrative list of such practices. In his report in 1990, the Director General listed examples of dubious trading practices known to the OFT which might be included in the list. Among these are 'the use of ambiguous descriptions' (the examples given include 'environmentally friendly batteries') and the 'use of literally true but misleading descriptions'.

Environmental claims could be regulated by a code of practice under a reformed part III of the Fair Trading Act, or possibly within the wording of the Act itself. Voluntary codes on their own do not work effectively to control abuses because they cannot be enforced. Giving statutory backing to a code solves this problem.

The Office of Fair Trading's proposals are directed towards achieving negotiated solutions to problems, backed up by civil action. As they stand, the OFT is proposing that it would be the sole enforcement authority, though the National Consumer Council thinks this would be better done jointly with trading standards officers. Under the proposals, a trader suspected of carrying on a course of conduct which is unfair, deceptive or misleading would be issued with a caution by the enforcement authorities, and only breach of this caution would precipitate civil action in the county court. This would make the problem of proving that claims were false or misleading much less crucial. If the case went to court, the standards of proof would be civil rather than criminal, that on the balance of probabilities the conduct has occurred.

The approach adopted under a reformed part III of the Fair Trading Act focuses on the practice or conduct of the trader making the claim, and would also include an illustrative list of the sorts of claims that could be misleading. Alternatively, this could form part of a code under the Act. This would be very helpful in providing guidance to traders, and the courts. It could be developed in consultation with industry, trading standards, consumer organisations and academics and with reference to the advertising codes to ensure a consistency of treatment of claims wherever they arise.

Using a reformed part III of the Fair Trading Act would be a creative and innovative means of dealing with misleading environmental claims, and might prove in practice not to be very costly, once a system had been established and some guidelines drawn up for those wanting to make claims. It does, however, depend on amending primary legislation, for which time must be found in the government's legislative programme. The Department of Trade and Industry has advised us that, though there was a manifesto commitment to this long-considered measure, no time will be found for it in the current programme. In dealing with environmental claims under this heading, however, the government could be seen to be legislating to fulfil two long-standing commitments: to tackle environmental claims and to reform part III of the Fair Trading Act. The additional merit would be that it would also deal with other abuses which current legislation cannot deal with effectively, and it would not impact on traders who were trading fairly. It would not be a technical barrier to trade.

Appendix 1

The shopping survey

As part of our brief from the Department of the Environment, the National Consumer Council was asked to find out how far consumers are affected by false or misleading environmental claims or statements about goods and services. It therefore was important that we establish what claims are currently being made on packaged goods and on labels attached to appliances, furniture and other items. We commissioned the Consumers' Association shopping unit to identify products with environmental claims, to record the wording and a description of the packaging, and to buy a selection of them or to obtain product literature where appropriate. This appendix is a report on the claims they recorded.

Consumers' Association employs shoppers to buy the products tested in *Which?* reports. Four shoppers, who had extensive experience in work of this kind, each spent four days shopping in mid-July 1995. One shopper was based in Leeds and shopped only for groceries. One was based in Bromley and Croydon and concentrated on high street chains and grocers not covered in Leeds. One was based in Hertfordshire and looked only at gardening and DIY products. Finally, one was based in Nottingham and covered white goods and furniture.

I.   Environmental claims on high street products and groceries

Claim: no harmful ingredients

Product and claim	*Brand*

1. Hairspray

'Contains NO CFC propellant alleged to damage ozone, Environmentally responsible.' *Logo:* a hand holding the sun and a leaf.	Asda own brand
'Does not contain CFCs which damages ozone.'	Sunsilk
'Ozone friendly.' 'Does not contain CFCs which damages ozone.'	Studio Line fixing spray by l'Oreal
'CFC free.'	Silvikrin
'CFC free.'	Alberto VO5
'No CFCs which damage the environment.'	Elnette
'CFC FREE. Does not contain CFCs which damage the ozone layer.' *Logo:* the world. Also states 'CFC FREE'.	Boots
'No CFCs.'	Harmony
Logo: the world encircled by the wording 'OZONE SAFE'.	Cossack

Product and claim	Brand

2. Styling mousse

'Contains NO CFC propellant alleged to damage ozone, Environmentally responsible.'　　　　　　　　　　Asda brand

Logo: hand holding sun and leaf.

'CFC FREE. Does not contain CFCs which damage the ozone layer.'　　　　　　　　　　Boots
Logo: the world. Also states 'CFC FREE'.

'The propellant used in this aerosol is a Butane/Propane blend.'　　　　　　　　　　Safeway own brand
Logo: abstract logo stating 'CFC FREE'.

'Does not contain propellants alleged to damage the ozone layer.'　　　　　　　　　　Flex

3. Shaving foam

'Contains NO CFC propellant alleged to damage ozone.'　　　　Asda own brand
Logo: hand holding sun and leaf.

'This product does not contain CFCs which are known to cause ozone depletion.'　　　　　　　　　　Tesco own brand
Logo: a heart.

'Ozone friendly, contains NO CFC propellant alleged to damage ozone.'　　　　　　　　　　Asda shave gell

'NO CFCs.'　　　　　　　　　　Cussons

'CFC Free.'　　　　　　　　　　Wilkinson Sword

Product and claim	Brand

3. Shaving foam continued

'CFC Free.'

Logo: the world.

Palmolive

4. Antiperspirant deodorant

'Contains NO CFC propellant alleged to damage ozone, Environmentally responsible.'

Logo: a hand holding the sun and a leaf.

Asda own brand

'This product does not contain CFCs which are known to cause ozone depletion.'

Logo: a heart.

Tesco own brand

'Does not contain CFCs which damage ozone.'

Brut

'NO CFCs.'

Imperial Leather

'NO CFCs.'

Cussons

'NO CFCs.'

Lady Mitchum

'NO CFCs.'

Sure

'CFC free.'

Charlie

'CFC free.'

Natural Plus

'CFC free.'

Soft and Gentle

'CFC free.'

Mum

'CFC free' (in three languages).

Harvard

Product and claim	*Brand*

4. Antiperspirant deodorant continued

'CFC FREE. Does not contain CFCs which damage the ozone layer.'   Boots
Logo: the world. Also states 'CFC FREE'.

'Ozone safe.'   Arrid
Logo: a pierced white disc.

5. Body spray

'This product does not contain CFCs which are known to cause ozone depletion.'   Tesco own brand
Logo: a heart.

'NO CFCs.'   Cussons

'NO CFCs.'   Impulse

'CFC free.'   Coty

'CFC FREE. Does not contain CFCs which damage the ozone layer.'   Boots
Logo: the world. Also states 'CFC FREE'.

6. Fly and wasp killer

'Contains NO CFCs.'   Raid
Logo: the sky with a pale blue colour and a dark blue colour divided by a white arc. Also states 'NO CFCs'.

7. Insecticide

'Does not contain CFCs.'   Rapid

Product and claim	*Brand*

8. Outdoor insect repellent

'Contains NO CFCs.' Raid

Logo: the sky with a pale blue colour and a dark blue colour divided by a white arc. Also states 'NO CFCs'.

9. Ant and cockroach killer

'Contains NO CFCs.' Raid

Logo: the sky with a pale blue colour and a dark blue colour divided by a white arc. Also states 'NO CFCs'.

10. Wasp nest destroyer

'Contains NO CFCs.' Raid

Logo: the sky with a pale blue colour and a dark blue colour divided by a white arc. Also states 'NO CFCs'.

11. Air freshener

'CFC FREE.' Asda own brand

'Contains no CFCs.' Glade

'NO CFCs.' Neutrafresh

'NO CFCs.' Sainsbury's own brand

'NO CFCs.' Air Wick Neutrair

Logo: the sky with a pale blue colour and a dark blue colour divided by a white arc.

Product and claim	*Brand*

11. Air freshener continued

'Non Aerosol.'

'Neutradol spray does not contain any hazardous
propellant (gas), and is therefore a non-aerosol product
and "ozone friendly".'

Logo: the world encircled by the wording 'CFC FREE.'
and 'OZONE FRIENDLY'.

Neutradol

Logo: the sky with a pale colour and a dark
colour divided by a white arc. Also states
'Contains no propellant alleged to DAMAGE OZONE'.

Astral Nice 'n'
Fresh

12. Polish

'Contains NO CFC propellant alleged to damage ozone,
Environmentally responsible.'
Logo: hand holding sun and leaf.

Asda own brand

'NO CFCs.'

Mr Sheen

'NO CFCs.'

Glade

'NO CFCs.'

Sainsbury's own brand

'New aerosol uses air as the only propellant.'
'Environmental information
Contains no CFCs.'
Logo: the sky with a pale blue colour and a dark blue
colour divided by a white arc. Also states 'NO CFCs'.

Sparkle

Product and claim	*Brand*

12. Polish continued

'New aerosol uses air as the only propellant.' — Pledge

'Environmental information

Contains no CFCs.'

'The new process developed by SC Johnson uses the natural strength of air as the only propellant. The air is pumped into the can in the same way as a bicycle tyre. The efficiency and practicality of the aerosol is maintained. This new generation of aerosol gives the same performance as traditional sprays while respecting the environment.'

Logo: the sky with a pale colour and a dark colour divided by a white arc. Also states 'NO CFCs'.

'This product does not contain CFCs which are known — Tesco's own brand
to cause ozone depletion.'

Logo: a heart.

13. Cleaning mousse

Logo: the world. Also the wording 'CFC FREE'. — Jif mousse

14. Spray paint

'Contains no fluorocarbons.' — Plastikote

'Ozone friendly.' 'Lead free'. — Decorative

Logo: the sky, with sun and clouds.

15. Batteries

'Source Reduction. We design our batteries to minimise the — Rayovac/Vidor
use of toxic materials and we minimise the use of materials
overall in our packaging. Our Higher Power Heavy Duty Batteries
are manufactured with a Mercury/Cadmium Free Formula.'

Logo: states 0% mercury/cadmium, circled by the wording
'respecting the environment'.

Product and claim   *Brand*

Claim: made from recycled material

Paper

1. Kitchen towel

'Reduces the amount of waste which is landfilled.'   Tesco's recycled
Packaging colour: green.   kitchen towel

2. Toilet roll

'Nouvelle has always been the benchmark in quality for   Nouvelle
brands made from 100% recycled paper. And now,
following our policy of continuous improvement,
New Improved Nouvelle is better than ever
… Not only do you save trees when you buy New Improved
Nouvelle you also save water. This is because our
manufacturing processes are amongst the most advanced
and resource efficient in the world.'
Logo: World wrapped in toilet paper which carries the
wording 'Softer on the environment'. The logo is also
encircled by the statement 'made from 100% recycled paper'.

'Sainsbury's Greencare toilet tissue is manufactured   Sainsbury's
from 100% low grade waste paper. 80% of this is   Greencare
 recycled newspaper and 20% reycled magazines.   toilet tissue
Most of this waste would otherwise have been buried
or incinerated.'
Logo: Hand holding the world, surrounded by the
wording 'environment friendlier'.

'100% selected recycled paper. No bleaches, dyes or optical Wholefood SUMA
brighteners are used. Dioxin safe, no more than
environmental background level.'

Product and claim	Brand

2. Toilet roll continued

'Made from 100% Recycled Paper.
When you buy Sainsbury's Revive you are helping to make a more effective use of natural resources because Revive is manufactured from 100% recycled paper.'
Logo: hand holding the world, encircled by the wording 'environment friendlier'.

Sainsbury's Revive

3. Sanitary towels

'Environment friendly. This product contains fluff pulp which is made with concern for the environment.
Asda Press-on Towels ... are Environment Friendly, containing fluff pulp which is made using a process considered to be less harmful to the environment.'
Logo: the sun and the sea and a hand holding a leaf.

Asda Press-on towels

4. Envelopes

Logo: Mobius loop, 100% recycled.
Imagery: a tree.

Recycle

5. Memo block

'In the interest of conservation, this product has been made from an obsolete map.'
'Breathing new life into waste paper products.'

Geo stationery

6. Parcel wrapping pack

'Recycled.'

Safewrap Homecare products

Product and claim   *Brand*

7. Paper napkins

'Made from 100% Recycled Paper.'   Sainsbury's
'These napkins are made from 100% recycled paper and
are not chlorine bleached.'
Logo: a hand holding the world encircled by the wording
'Environment Friendly'.
Imagery: a leaf; waves; green mountains.

8. Cereal boxes

'This packaging uses 70% recycled board.'   Sainsbury's
Logo: a hand holding the world, encircled by
the Mobius loop.

Claim: sustainable (*)

1. Stationery

'Environmentally Friendly From Managed Forests   Hammond Gower
For Every Tree Felled Two Are Replaced.'   publications
Logo: the world protected by two hands, encircled by the
wording 'Printed on environmentally conscious paper'.

'Paper used to produce this card and envelope is   Hallmark Cards
biodegradable and comes from replanted forests
in Europe and North America.'

2. Document wallet

'Manufactured in Great Britain from sustainable   Concord
forest sources.'   Document wallets

* More claims on 'sustainability' appear on other products which were
bought in DIY and garden shops. (For these, see pages 159-160.)

Product and claim	*Brand*

3. Toilet paper

As with the manufacture of all DIXCEL products no wood
pulp from tropical rainforests is ever used and we do
not add optical brightening agents.

Dixcel

4. Sketch pad

'Product made with paper from a sustainable forest.'

WH Smith

5. Parcel wrapping pack

'Recycled.'

Safewrap

Logo: a tree beside which is the statement 'Safewrap
Kraft paper is made from recycled paper
pulp originating from renewable forests only.'

Homecare products

Claim: no bleach or no optical brighteners

1. Tissues

'Produced from renewable resources. Not chlorine'.

Kleenex

'Bleached using low chlorine process
More environmentally responsible than other methods.'

Tesco's own brand

2. Baby wipes

'Bleached without the use of chlorine gas.'
Logo: the world surrounded by the wording
'Caring for the environment'.

Boots Baby
Lotion wipes

'These wipes have been bleached in accordance with strict
environmental standards.'

Boots Baby cloth
wipes

Product and claim	*Brand*

3. Paper napkins

'These napkins are made from 100% recycled paper and are not chlorine bleached.'

Logo: a hand holding the world encircled by the wording 'Environment Friendly'.

Imagery: a leaf; waves; green mountains.

Sainsbury's

4. Washing powder

'No chlorine bleaches.' 'No optical brighteners.'

Logo: Sunflower and bee encircled by the wording 'The BIO D Company'.

BioD

'No chlorine bleach.' 'Green Clean does not produce organic chlorine compounds during degradation. Chlorine may be very toxic in some circumstances.' 'No optical brighteners.' 'Green Clean reduces the risk of skin irritation and damage to important microorganisms.'

Green Clean

5. Toilet paper

'Nonchlorine bleached.'

'... Chlorine has been traditionally used to help meet the high standards of brightness, strength and cleanliness expected by you the customer. However, our technology now enables to meet these standards with a TOTALLY CHLORINE FREE bleaching process.'

'Best of all Dixcel Nonchlorine Bleached bathroom tissue offers you the choice of a quality tissue ...,
whilst helping to protect our environment.'

'As with the manufacture of all DIXCEL products ...
we do not add optical brightening agents.'

Imagery: green and blue pack, figuring a bird, a butterfly, a fish, a leaf.

Dixcel

Product and claim   *Brand*

Claim: method of production

Product: food

1. Tuna

Logo: shows a leaping dolphin and states 'dolphin friendly'.   Princes

Logo: a heart with the picture of the world. Around it are   Tesco
the words 'Dolphin friendly'.

2. Flour

'Organic.' 'For more than a decade Doves Farm Foods have   Doves Farm
sold organic foods which are produced on farms in accordance
with the published standards of the Soil Association.
Organic farmers develop soil fertility by growing different
crops in rotation and returning plant and animal residues to
the soil within a carefully managed ecosystem.'
'Produced to Soil Association organic standards.'
Logo: the Soil Association Organic Standard logo.

3. Sugar

'Billington's Golden Caster sugar is an unrefined cane   Billington's Golden
sugar which replaces white caster sugar. It is carefully
produced from raw sugar cane by a simple, energy efficient
process on the tropical island of Mauritius. So there is no
need for the additional chemical involved in refining the
sugar. Golden Caster is unrefined, unbleached and
therefore retains its natural colour and delicate flavour.
No additives. No colouring.'
Logo: Canes surrounded by the words: 'Unbleached'
'Unrefined' 'Raw cane'.

Product and claim   *Brand*

4. Water

'The Hildon source lies deep within chalk hills which   Hildon
border the Test Valley in Hampshire, fully protected
from the environment.'

5. Cereals

'Grown with conservation in mind.'   Mornflake
'Natural pure food and stone ground too.'
'No additives preservatives or sweeteners.'
'A delicious breakfast the old fashioned way.'

'Jordan Oats are grown to the Special Standard of the   Jordan Porridge
Guild of Conservation Grade Food producers. They   Oats
are grown without chemicals which leave a toxic
residue in the crop or soil. So the Oats are purer,
and the land reverts to a healthier balance. Farms
are independently inspected to maintain quality
standards.'
Logo: stylised cereal in shape of a tick in circle.
wording 'Conservation Grade.'

Claim: biodegradable

1. Shampoo
'Biodegradable.'   Faith in Nature

'Biodegradable.'   Flex

2. Conditioner
'Biodegradable.'   Faith in Nature

Product and claim	*Brand*

3. Washing powder and liquids

'Less resources wash for wash. Daz Ultra products use
30% less resources than conventional powders.
Biodegradable: The cleaning agents in this product are
broken down by natural products.'

Daz

'Environmental information
Less powder per wash. New Ariel Future uses more
effective ingredients which allow you to use
less powder per wash than with Ariel Ultra.
Biodegradable. The cleaning agents in Ariel Future are
broken down by natural processes.'
Logo: WWF Panda. 'Ariel Future is working with WWF
towards a better environment.'

Ariel Future

'To help safeguard the environment the detergents used
in this product are biodegradable and are broken down
into harmless materials by sewage treatment and
natural process.'
Logo: Mobius loop: in its centre is a hand holding
the world.

Sainsbury's
Novon

'Environment.'
'The surface active ingredients in Biological Persil
liquid are biodegradable and break down rapidly into
harmless substances.'
Logo: a green valley with a river and the rising sun,
encircled by an arrow which contains the wording
'Environmental information'.

Biological Persil
Concentrated liquid

Product and claim   *Brand*

3. Washing powder and liquids continued

'Environmental information.'   Asda's Integra
'Integra's surface active ingredients are biodegradable and
break down rapidly and naturally into harmless substances.'

'Environmental information.   Bold
Biodegradable. The cleaning agents in this product are
broken down by natural process.'
Logo: a tree with a river and birds, encircled by an arrow
 which contains the wording 'Environmental information'.

'Environmental information
<u>Product</u> Plant Based ingredients. This product is derived   Down to Earth
from renewable plants (palm and coconut oils); Phosphate   concentrated
free. Biodegradable: This product is classified readily   automatic
biodegradable by the OECD Protocol 301E, which means   liquid
its molecules break down rapidly and completely into
harmless substances (water and carbon dioxide).'
Logo: the world.

'All ingredients are completely biodegradable within   Green Clean
3-5 days. Using Green Clean as an alternative can help
reduce pollution and thereby protect nature.'

Product and claim	Brand

3. Washing powder and liquids continued

'Environmental information.' <u>Biodegradable</u>: To safeguard the environment the surface active ingredients of Radion are biodegradable and break down rapidly by natural processes into harmless substances.

Logos: (a) Mobius loop; (b) a green valley with a river and the rising sun, encircled by an arrow which contains the wording 'Environmental information'.

Radion automatic

'Highly biodegradable ingredients: This product is based only on highly effective minerals and plant based ingredients which biodegrade quickly with a minimum impact on the environment. Plant based surfactants (ionic and anionic tenside) lose all tensio-activity within 3-5 days (OECD Screening Test). Soap is fully biodegradable within 3 days (EMPA-Test).'

Logo: a leaf in a square.

Ecover concentrated washing powder

'Phosphate free Enzyme free Perfume free.'
Logo: Sunflower and bee encircled by the wording.

'The BIO D Company.'

BioD

Product and claim   *Brand*

3. Washing powder and liquids continued

'No phosphates. Green Clean does not promote the   Green Clean
growth of algae which causes oxygen deficiency in
the water, harming fish and aqueous plants.
No zeolites. Green Clean avoids the risk of depositing toxic
aluminium in water and soil in places such as Scandinavia and
Canada and also in areas of naturally soft water. No NTA or
EDTA.Green Clean helps to protect our drinking water from
lead and other polluting metals. NTA was formerly the
alternative to phosphates in detergents. It is now prohibited
in several countries because both NTA and EDTA bind
heavy metals. No enzymes. Green Clean reduces the risk of
allergies and avoids the use of gene technology.
No synthetic colours or perfumes. Both of these have
petro-chemical origins and may be toxic. They are harmful
to water organisms, irritate skin, and degrade slowly. We
only use genuine essential oils and no colouring agents at all.'

'Environment Information. Concentrated powder: Tesco Green Choice
This formulation is concentrated, and so uses less   Ultra Concentrated
chemicals and packaging than standard powders.   automatic powder
Vegetable derived surfactants: The soap in this
product has all been derived from renewable vegetable
resources, rather than nonrenewable fossil fuel.
No Phosphates: phosphates have been excluded from this
product, as there is some concern that an excess of
phosphates may lead to an increased growth of algae.
This could deprive fish and other organisms of the oxygen
and sunlight needed for their survival.'
Logo: Heart containing the world.

Product and claim	*Brand*

3. Washing powder and liquids continued

'The detergents used in this product are biodegradable.' — St Michael Hand Wash liquid

4. Washing up liquid

'Biodegradable The surfactants in this product are biodegradable.'
Imagery: a heart. — Tesco's own brand

'This product contains biodegradable detergents.' — Asda's own brand

'Contains only biodegradable detergents.' — Sainsbury's concentrated lemon

'Readily biodegradable.'
'Down to Earth is a range of specially formulated cleaning products based on ingredients derived from natural renewable sources. This ensures effective grease cutting action and excellent results whilst respecting the environment and caring for your family. Helpful environmental information. Readily biodegradable is a classification given to materials that have passed stringent OECD tests to ensure they biodegrade rapidly and completely. Natural based cleaners means that Down to Earth's cleaning agents are derived from naturally occurring plant sources (Coconut Oil) which are renewable.' — Down to Earth

'Sainsbury's Greencare range of cleaning products is specially formulated with priority given to the environment. Wherever possible, we use biodegradable materials from renewable resources.'
Logo: a hand holding the world, encircled by the wording 'environment friendlier'. — Sainsbury's Greencare

Product and claims	*Brand*

5. Fabric conditioner

'Biodegradable
The softener in Asda's fabric conditioner is biodegradable
which means that it is broken down by natural processes.'

Asda own brand

'Environmental information. Biodegradability: the
softening agents in Lenor Ultra Plus are biodegradable.'

Lenor Ultra Plus

'Sainsbury's Greencare range of cleaning products is
specially formulated, with priority given to care for
the environment. Wherever possible, we use biodegradable
materials from renewable resources.
Vegetable based detergents. Biodegradable fragrance.'
Logo: hand holding the world, encircled by the wording
'environment friendlier.'

Sainsbury's
Greencare

6. Toilet cleaner/tablets

'This product contains biodegradable detergents.'

Asda own brand

'As with all our products only biodegradable
surfactants are used.'

Tesco's Blue
germicidal
toilet flush

'The surfactants in this product are biodegradable.'

Odour Neutralising
Premium Lavatory
Freshener

Logo: the world, encircled by the wording 'Environmental
information'. See back. 'Environmental information'
'Bloo uses biodegradable detergent and recycled card.'

Bloo

Product and claim	Brand

7. Disinfectant

'This product contains biodegradable detergents.'   Asda own brand

8. Household cleaners

'This product contains biodegradable detergents.'   Asda own brand

'Environmental information. Biodegradable.   Jif
To safeguard the environment, Jif's surface active
ingredients are biodegradable and break down rapidly
by natural process into harmless substances.'
Logo: a green valley with a river and the rising
sun, encircled by an arrow, containing the wording
'Environmental information.'

'Environmental information. Biodegradable.   Jif kitchen
To safeguard the environment, Jif's surface active
ingredients are biodegradable and break down rapidly
by natural process into harmless substances.'
Logo: a green valley with a river and the rising
sun, encircled by an arrow, containing the wording
'Environmental information'.

'Environmental information. Biodegradable.   Jif mousse
To safeguard the environment, Jif's surface active
ingredients are biodegradable and break down rapidly
by natural process into harmless substances.'

'Environmental information.'   Flash
'The cleaning agents in this product are biodegradable
(they are broken down into harmless materials).'

Product and claim	Brand

8. Household cleaners continued

'Environmental information.'
'The cleaning agents in this product are biodegradable
(they are broken down into harmless materials).'

Excel Flash
Bathroom cleaner

'Environmental information.'
'Ajax cream contains amongst other ingredients: less
than 5% Anionic surfactants, Nonionic surfactants.
These are biodegradable and break down by natural
processes into harmless substances.'

Ajax

'Environmental information.'
'Ibcol contains biodegradable detergent, this breaks
down into substances harmless to the environment by
way of natural processes and sewage treatment.'

Ibcol

'HIGHLY BIODEGRADABLE. This product contains
highly effective minerals and plant based ingredients
which biodegrade quickly with minimum impact on the
environment. Plant based surfactants (anionic tenside)
lose all tensio-activity within 3-5 days (OECD Screening
nonionic tenside Test). Sugar based surfactants
are rapidly biodegradable (OECD Test 301D).'
Logo: a leaf.

Ecover cream
cleaner

9. Dishwasher liquid

'Easy on the environment
No phosphates preserving rivers, lakes and streams.
All ingredients are fully biodegradable or inorganic
no harmful chemicals left behind. Vegan.'

Clear Spring

Product and claim	*Brand*

10. Bleach

'Environmental information. The bleach ingredients in Domestos are rapidly broken down after use. The surface active ingredients in Domestos are biodegradable and break down rapidly by natural process into harmless substances.'

Logo: a green valley with a river and the rising sun, encircled by an arrow, containing the wording 'Environmental information See Back'.

Domestos

'Environmental Information.'
Parozone Thick power Bleach is degradable and breaks down in the environment to harmless materials.'

Logo: a split world with the words 'Environmental information See Back.'

Parozone

'Environmental Information. Parozone Bleach block does not contain PDCB. Parozone Bleach Block uses biodegradable detergents and recycled card.'

Logo: a split world with the words Environmental information See Back'.

Parozone bleach block

11. Stain remover

'Environmental information.'
'Formula contains surfactants which are up to 90% biodegradable according to recognised tests.'

Shout

12. Greeting cards

'Paper used to produce this card and envelope is biodegradable and comes from replanted forests in Europe and North America.'

Hallmark Cards

Product and claim   *Brand*

Claim: packaging made from recycled/recyclable materials

1. Hand wash liquid bottle

Logo: 'der grüne Punkt', mobius loop with HDPE   St Michael Hand Wash
wording, number 2.   liquid for wool and
                                                          silks

2. Bleach bottle

'This bottle is made of Polyethelene and contains more   Domestos
than 25% recycled plastic.'
Logo: a green valley with a river and the rising sun,
encircled by an arrow, which contains the wording
'Environmental information See Back'.

3. Water bottle

Logo: Mobius loop with PET wording, number 1.   Buxton

4. Washing up liquid bottle

'Label and bottle are made of HDPE cap of PP.   Ecover
All are 100% recyclable.'
Logo: Mobius loop with HDPE wording, number 2.

5. Household cleaner bottle

'Label and bottle are made of HDPE cap of PP.   Ecover
Logo: Mobius loop with HDPE wording, number 2.

6. Antibacterial disinfectant bottle

'Ibcol is packaged in recyclable materials.'   Ibcol

Product and claim	*Brand*

7. Conditioner bottle

Logo: Mobius loop, number 2.

Freeman Botanical conditioner

8. Shampoo bottle

'Product in recyclable packaging.'

Flex

9. Stain removing spray

Logo: Mobius loop with HDPE wording, number 2.

Shout

10. Aftersun spray

Logo: Mobius Loop with PP wording, number 5.

Body Shop

11. Recycled refuse sacks

'Guarantee: contains a minimum of recycled waste, a mix of industrial, supermarket and consumer recovered materials which would otherwise have been largely buried or incinerated.' 'Contains genuine recycled material to help preserve natural resources.'
Logo: Circling Arrow indicates 'recycled' 50%.

Kitchen Pride

12. Furniture spray

'Container is made from 25% recycled material.'

Sparkle

'Container is made from 25% recycled material.'

Pledge

13. Air freshener

'Container is made from 25% recycled material.'

Haze

14. Batteries storage pack

'Ravoyac/Vidor Smart Pack uses 61% less plastic and 29% less paper than carded battery packages.'

Rayovac Vidor

Product and claim   *Brand*

15. Germicidal toilet flush wrapper

'Environment information   Tesco's Blue
Each block is wrapped in PVA film and then packed in
a cardboard and PVC pack. The cardboard used is made
from a minimum of 85% recycled board.'

16. Shaving foam

'Recyclable can.'   Palmolive
Logo: 'der grüne Punkt'.

17. Deodorant

Logo: 'der grüne Punkt'.   Harvard
                                                       by St Michael

18. Tuna can

'Steel recyclable.'   Tesco

19. Compost

'Packaging made from recyclable polythene.'   Levington
Logo: Mobius loop, number 4.

20. Washing powder

'Environmental information   Bold
Packaging. This pack is made from 80% recycled material.'
Logo: a tree with a river and birds, encircled by an
arrow, which contains the wording
'Environmental information'.

'This packaging uses 75% recycled board.'   Sainsbury's Novon
Logo: Mobius loop with a hand holding the world.

Product and claim	*Brand*

20. Washing powder continued

'Environmental information
Concentrated refill pack. Enables you to reuse your
bottle and reduce waste Recycled packaging.
This pack is made from 30% recycled cardboard.
Less waste. This carton is crushable, which
means it takes less space in landfill sites. It can be
incinerated without any danger to the environment.'
Logo: the world.

Down to Earth

'Environmental information. Packaging: The pack
contains recycled cardboard material and is recyclable.'
Logos: (a) Mobius loop; (b) a green valley with a river and
the rising sun, encircled by an arrow, which contains the
wording 'Environmental information'.

Radion

Logo: Mobius loop, 85% recycled cardboard.

Ecover

'Environment. This carton uses half the packaging material
of a 1L bottle. This carton is crushable for easy disposal.'
Logo: a green valley with a river and the rising sun,
encircled by an arrow, containing the wording
'Environmental information'.

Biological Persil
Concentrated liquid

'URTEKRAM is also proud to package in 100% recycled
cardboard.'
Logo: of 'der grüne Punkt' with its wording.

Green Clean

Recycled packaging. This box is made from at least 85%
recycled board. This carton contains a cardboard
scoop made from at least 85% recycled board.'
Logo: Heart containing the world.

Tesco Green
Choice Ultra
concentrated

Product and claim	Brand

21. Tampons
'For the environment fewer layers of packaging.' Lillets

22. Coffee pack
Logo: Mobius loop, with the wording 'recycled'. Cafedirect

23. Toilet tablet
Logo: the world, encircled by the wording Bloo
'Environmental information' See back.
'Environmental information.'
'Bloo uses biodegradable detergent and recycled card.'

'Environmental Information. Parozone Bleach block Parozone Extra
does not contain PDCB. Parozone Bleach Block uses Power Bleach
biodegradable detergents and recycled card.'
Logo: a split world 'Environmental information See Back.'

Claim: refill packs

1. Fabric conditioner refill
'Environmental information - Less waste: this Tesco's own brand
refill pack allows you to reuse your fabric
conditioner bottle again and again reducing the amount of
waste in the environment.'

Product and claim	Brand

2. Washing powder refill
'Ecorefill.'   Persil

'Environmental information. Concentrated refill pack.   Down to Earth
Enables you to reuse your bottle and reduce waste.
Recycled packaging. This pack is made from 30%
recycled cardboard. Less waste. This carton is crushable,
which means it takes less space in landfill sites. It can be
incinerated without any danger to the environment.'
Logo: the world.

3. Liquid detergent
'Environment. This carton uses half the packaging   Persil
 material of a 1L bottle. This carton is crushable
for easy disposal.'
Logo: a green valley with a river and the rising sun,
encircled by an arrow, which contains the wording
'Environmental information'.

4. Washing up liquid
'New Refill.'   Sainsbury's
'Refill your bottle Use less packaging.'   Concentrated Lemon

5. Baby wipes refill
'This pack uses approximately 80% less plastic by   Boots Baby Lotion
weight than the parent canister.'   Wipes

Logo: the world surrounded by the wording
'Caring for the environment'.

6. Stain removing spray
'Trigger can be reused on Shout refills.'   Shout

Product and claim   *Brand*

7. Various Body Shop products
'Please retain packaging for recycling.'   Body Shop

Claim: low energy usage

'Environmental information. Energy usage: the oxygen   Radion Biological
based bleaching system ensures excellent performance
at low temperatures, saving energy in heating the water.'
Logos: (a) Mobius loop; (b) a green valley with a river
and the rising sun, encircled by an arrow, containing the
words 'Environmental information'.

General statements on the impact on the environment

1. Nappies
'Ultra-thin means less raw materials, less   Kleenex
packaging and less to dispose of, thereby reducing   Ultrathin
impact on the environment.'
Symbol: Caring for the environment.

'For more information on our "environmental compatibility"   Pampers
write to ... or visit ...'

2. Tissues
'Working for quality and the environment.'   Andrex

3. Toilet roll
'Softer on the environment.'   Nouvelle

Product and claim	*Brand*

4. Washing powder

'Respects the environment.' 'see side panel for details.' — Down to Earth

'Ecover products are produced at the world's first ecological factory, a clean running plant that helps preserve the community while providing you with high quality products.' 'Effective products for people who care about a clean environment.' 'Ecover care about you and your environment and are committed to providing you with high performance products of high ecological value.'
Logo: Three green people (a family) in a row
The UN logo for outstanding environmental achievement. — Ecover

'Vegan. User friendly. All our products are made from renewable sources. Products for a cleaner environment.'
Logo: Sunflower and bee encircled by the wording 'The BIO D Company'. — BioD

'Washing ecologically safe.'
'After many enquiries and much research for all the ingredients necessary to produce a Green Clean vegetarian detergent, we are now proud to announce the washing powder of the future. URTEKRAM's goal is to introduce a detergent which is as gentle as possible to people and nature. Of course, you cannot solve all the pollution problems in the world just by buying Green Clean, but you can go a long way in the right direction.' — Green Clean

'Towards a cleaner environment.'
Logo: hand holding the world, encircled by the words 'environment friendlier.' — Sainsbury's Greencare

'No unnecessary ingredients.' — Tesco Green Choice Ultra Concentrated

Product and claim   *Brand*

5. Dishwasher liquid

'Easy on the environment.'   Clear Spring
'Faith in Nature.'

6. Household cleaner

'From the caring company. Ecover products are produced   Ecover
at the world's first ecological factory, a clean running plant
that helps preserve the community while providing you
with high quality products. For people who care.'
Logo: House with a green roof.
'Using Ecover products is one way to help preserve
the environment and show you care. We welcome your
comments, questions and suggestions through the
Ecover Washing line.'
Logo: Three green people (a family) in a row.
The UN logo for outstanding environmental
achievement.

7. Matches

'Green Tips. Travel. Keeping tyres at the correct   Cook's
pressure reduces fuel consumption and emissions,   Matches
makes driving safer and helps tyres last longer.
Under inflated tyres increase fuel consumption
by up to 5%.'

Product and claim	*Brand*

7. Matches continued

'Green Tips. For a better environment. We're all
aware of the threats to our environment caused by
acid rain, global warming and the greenhouse effect.
By changing our lifestyle in small ways, we can all
make a positive contribution to our environment,
from recycling our waste material to conserving energy
and the earth's natural resources. Bryant & May
has compiled a list of facts and figures on the
environment, and gives advice on how to be more
environmentally friendly at home, when travelling and
general hints on recycling.' 'For further information
send for the "GreenTips" Leaflet.'

Swan

8. Conditioner

Logo (a): the world wrapped by a tape stating
'Freeman cares'.
Logo (b): Mobius loop.

Freeman Botanical

Environmental statements on carrier bags

Claim   *Brand*

This bag is made from genuinely recycled plastic,   Sainsbury's
much of which comes from our own store waste.'
Logo: Mobius Loop.

'Please reuse this bag and help to protect the   Morrisons
environment.'

'To help save the earth's resources this bag contains   Mothercare
approximately 25% recycled polythene.'
Logo: a landscape with the sun, the hills, trees and the sea.

'Help protect the environment.'   Presto
'Please reuse this bag.'
'Worn or torn bags should not be used but can be
recycled.' 'Made with recycled material.'
Logo: Mobius loop.

'To help us save the environment's resources please   Boots
re-use this bag where possible.'

No environmental information found

Our shopper could not find any environmental information on Morrisons own
brands. Shopping in Presto (part of the Safeway Group), our shopper found
environmental information on polish, air freshener, hairspray and styling
mousse of Safeways own brands (see quotations). None of the other own
brands seen in the Presto shop carried any environmental information.

No environmental information was on any of the dishwasher powders or hair mousses sold in the Kwiksave and the Holland and Barrett store visited. Kwiksave's own brand products called 'No frills' had no environmental information on them. None of the foambaths in Kwiksave had any environmental information. The only manufacturer in Kwiksave to give environmental information on their shampoos and conditioners was Revlon.

Mr Muscle products had no environmental information on them.

In the Tesco shop visited, no environmental information was found on either dishwasher rinse aids or dishwasher salts or dishwasher powders the brands were:

Finish
Tesco's own brand
Fairy
Sun

None of the own brand dishwasher powders seen in the Marks and Spencers nor Asda mentioned the environment.

No environmental claims appeared on toilet rolls and tissues seen in the Marks and Spencer store visited.

In the Safeway store visited by our shopper there were no environmental information, claims or recycled symbols on any paper or plastic tableware.

Similarly, in the Woolworth store visited, the paper or plastic cups, party cups, serviettes, table cloths carried no environmental information. Such information, on the other hand, was found on Sainsbury's paper napkins.

Stores visited

Asda	Body Shop
Boots	Holland & Barrett
Kwiksave	Marks & Spencers
Morrisons	Natural Foodstore
Presto	Safeway
J. Sainsbury	Tesco
WH Smith	Waitrose
Woolworths	

II. Wooden home furniture

Comments

No environmental labels appeared on any of the furniture seen in the shops. Only one of the shop managers and owners recalled ever seeing any reference to environmental matters. The only labels on the furniture were about fire retardancy.

In one shop, manufacturers' labels (such as fire retardancy, stain resistance, guarantee) had been removed and only the shop's own price was shown. Among the material that had been removed one label (Wades) and one brochure (Ercol's) had environmental claims.

In another shop, Jessop & Son, no labels were found on the furniture, but there were two brochures (Ducal and Bradley), which did mention the environment. Jessop & Son is part of John Lewis Partnership. It is now apparently the firm's policy to support only those manufacturers who buy wood from sites where replanting of the timber resources takes place.

Furniture was usually delivered plastic wrapped. The packaging also showed no claims about recyclability.

Stores visited in Nottingham
Sail Bros Ltd
Homecare Furniture
Bulwell Furnishers
Thorpes of Ilkeston
Kingsbury Interiors
Wades Furnishing
Cantors PLC
Hopewells Furnishers
Jessop & Son

III. Garden furniture and DIY

Comments

No environmental statements were made on the vast majority of the products our shopper looked at. These included:

Sherwood pine range
Chindwell doors
Home doors
Woodcraft doors
Nordic softwood pack
Premium wood
Polar Patio doors
Larch-lap fencing, posts, trellis and sheds
Pan Gardening trellis
Smallford sheds
Alton greenhouses
Stirrwood garden furniture
Pan and Forrest trellis, wooden doors, wooden furniture.

The only environmental statements found were:

Homebase pineboard: 'The wood used in Homebase pineboard is sourced from the mature forests of North Europe, where cold climates produce slow growth offering a densely grained wood with smaller knots and greater strength'.

And, the following statement appeared in the Forest brochure: 'All timber produced in Forest products is sourced from managed sustainable forests'.

More specific environmental information was given in other cases:

Kwila Furniture South Western Manufacturing: 'Kwila occurs in Northern Australia, New Guinea and Eastern Indonesia. The timber is produced in accordance with the International Tropical Timber Organisation (ITTO) guidelines for sustainable management of "natural tropical forests" and from established plantations in accordance with the strategy outlined at the tenth session of the ITTO.'

Again, more specific information on the source of the wood was given by Barlow Tyrie garden furniture, which also provided a brochure: 'All Barlow Tyrie products are manufactured from teakwood obtained from strictly controlled plantations in Java, Indonesia, a recognized sustainable resource. Because of this long term use of plantation teak, Barlow Tyrie products have been approved by the "Friends of the Earth" and are listed in their "Good Wood Guide".'

Stores visited
Do It All
Homebase
B&Q
Notcutt Garden Centre

IV. White goods: fridges, freezers and washing machines

Comments

A relatively small number of fridges & freezers displayed stickers with the following statements:

'100% CFC Free.'

'CFC Free' (in 4 languages).

'CFC Free' (in 3 languages).

'CFC Free cooling.'

'CFC Free.'

'Ozone friendlier.'

'100% CFC Free. No damage to ozone layer' (in 4 languages).

'BEKO 100% CFC Free to protect our environment.'

'ECO designed with the environment in mind. Economical. Ecological.'

Leaflets with similar statements were also available.

The majority of fridges and freezers are in fact CFC free. Fewer labels indicating CFC free are being attached by manufacturers as customers assume that all fridges and freezers are CFC free anyway. However this is not yet entirely true, and certainly may not apply to older stocks. Any older stock that is not CFC free must be cleared by a date to be specified by the European Union. As far as manufacturers labels are concerned, it is also true that shop owners often remove them, preferring to display the new energy label. All these appliances will shortly have energy labelling on them.

Labels which appeared on washing machines carried the following statements:

'ECO Friendly.'

'OKO The Green Machine.'

'ECO Safe plus Micro Filtration.'

'CFC Free.'

Stores visited in Nottingham

Comet

Jessop & Son

Electricity & Superstore

Miller Bros, Victoria Retail Park, Netherfield, Nottingham

Curry's Ltd

Home Power

Norweb Electrical

Greater Nottingham Co-op Society

V. Insulation

The following environmental statement appeared in Supawrap loft insulation: 'Owens Corning is a member of Eurisol which supports the government's campaign to combat global warming'. It is accompanied by a logo featuring a house and a world symbol underlined by the statement: 'Helping the earth begins at home'.

Other environmental statements which appeared were the following:

Texas Pipe insulation: 'CFC Free.' 'No CFC content Ozone friendlier.'

Rockwool: 'Energy saver' 'Caring for the environment' 'Conserving Britain's bats' with full details about bat conservation and the Wildlife and Countryside Act 1981.

None of the other products our shopper looked at carried any statements:

Radiator reflector
Loft insulation
Pilkington Supamat All Round Home Insulation
Homebase Loft Insulation
Split Pipe Insulation
Mayplas Kitemarked Cylinder Jacket.

Stores visited
Homebase
Texas
B&Q
Do It All

VI. Garden composts

Most of the environmental statements on compost packagings referred to the source of the compost. Some packaging carried a marketing logo to reinforce the environmental nature of the product.

However, most packagings carried no environmental statements:

Homebase Compost
Zeneca Forest Bark
Ayletts Multipurpose Compost
Erin Multipurpose Compost
Notcutt Peat
Notcutt Irish Moss Peat
Notcutt Ornamental Bark
Do It All own brand compost
Tunstall brand
Supamix Topsoil
Keri Compost

Some packagings, referred only to the compost being 'organic':

Super Natural Multipurpose organic houseplant compost
Betagro Organic Compost
Greenvale farm organic plant feed

The environmental statements which appeared were the following:
Bio Multicompost: 'Peat free'.
Symbol: 'tick' of approval.

Shamrock Irish moss peat and B&Q Houseplant compost: 'Peat contained in this product has not been harvested from areas of scientific interest'.
Logo: a leaf symbol.

Shamrock Horticulture provided extensive environmental information on the sourcing of the peat contained in the compost in their brochure: '... No Shamrock peat or compost products contain peat harvested from areas of scientific interest. Shamrock's parent company in Ireland, Bord na Mona, is working closely with environmental groups to ensure all its peatlands of nature conservation interest are maintained ...'

Premier Multipurpose Compost: 'Peat in this product has not been harvested from areas of scientific interest'.
Logo: a flower symbol.

Fisons rich dark peat: 'Environment conservation peat producers code of practice'.
Logo: hands holding tree of life symbol.
Packaging: made from LDPE.
Recycling symbol, grade 4.

Gardenman Fresh Moss: 'Collected under licence'.

Gardenstore compost: 'Packaging made from recyclable polythene'.

Westland Multipurpose compost: 'Recyclable polythene'.
Recycling symbol, grade 4.

Levington Houseplant potting compost: 'Packaging made from recyclable polythene'.
Recycling symbol, grade 4.

J. Arthur Bower's New Horizon Compost: 'Peat free'; 'An environmentally friendly product'.

J. Arthur Bower's Compost Maker: 'Puts natural goodness back into the earth'.

Godwins Multipurpose Compost: 'Somerset Trust for Nature conservation'
'Made from coconut fibre and lignite'.
Logo: a badger.

Sunshine Africa cocoa shell: 'A byproduct of chocolate manufacture. A naturally renewable resource'.

Stores visited
B&Q
Aylett Nurseries
Do It All
Texas
Notcutt Garden Centre
Homebase
Robert Dyas Hardware store

VII. Insecticides and fungicides

Not much environmental information was given on the products themselves. The only environmental statements made appeared on:

Fisons Fungicide Insect Killer
B&Q Complete Insecticide Spray
Both were said to be 'biodegradable'.

Safety measures for the disposal of the product were given by:

Fisons Fungicide Insect Killer
B&Q Complete Insecticide Spray
B&Q Antkiller
B&Q Garden Fungicide spray
Vitax Pest Killer
Cuprinol Fungicide
Murphy Traditional Copper Fungicide
Doff Ant Killer
Growing Success Antkiller
Homebase Antkiller
Homebase pestgun
Rentokil wasp nest killer

The safety measures mentioned were:

'Apply away from fish.'
'Empty container thoroughly and dispose of safely.'
'Dangerous to fish, birds, bees and pets.'
'Empty container thoroughly or dispose of safely.'
'Harmful to fish or aquatic life.'
'Dangerous to fish and other aquatic life.'
'Do not contaminate watercourses or ground.'
'Do not contaminate surface water or ditches.'

'Do not contaminate ponds or streams.'

'Dispose of safely.'

'Dispose of used packaging safely.'

'This material and its container must be disposed of in a safe way'.

Information on the impact of the packaging included:

PY Garden Insecticide: 'Contains no propellants alleged to damage ozone'.

Vitax Pest Killer: 'Contains no propellant alleged to damage ozone'.

Stores visited

B&Q

Aylett Nurseries

Do It All

Texas

Notcutt Garden Centre

Homebase

Robert Dyas hardware store

VIII. Paints and varnishes

Comments referring to the ingredients of the products appeared on:

Rustin's paint

Helmsman varnish

Dulux

Crown

Berger

The comments were:

'No lead added.'

'Contains no lead.'

'Contains no added lead.'

'Contains no added solvents or lead.'

Comments referring to the packaging appeared on:

Ronseal brushing wax

Ronseal varnish

Berger

Dulux Refill

Do it all paint

Hammerite paint aerosols

Texas paint

B&Q

Premier

Plastikote decorative

Homebase

Homebase Refill pack

Claims

'Recyclable steel.'

WWF seal of approval - brochure gives sponsorship details.

'Recyclable' with magnet symbol.

'This can contains 25% recycled steel.'

'This can is made from 25% recycled steel and should be recycled.'

'Please recycle.'

'Take to the local household waste disposal site.'

'When empty, this refill pack may be disposed of safely through normal waste collection or handling.'

'This aerosol does not contain CFCs.'

'Ozone friendly.'

'Contains no fluorocarbons.'

Safety measures on the disposal of the product: 'Do not empty into drains or watercourses':

Dulux

Crown

Berger

No statements or advice:

Paints

Polycell Evenceil and International paints

Hammerite smooth finish paints

Varnishes

Colron

Ronseal

Sadolin

Texas

Homebase varnish

Wickes

Stores visited

Robert Dyas Hardware Store

Do It All

B&Q

Wickes

Appendix 2

Symbols and logos: general

This appendix is reproduced from the sheets shown to the shoppers who took part in our group discussions.

We're sorry about the reproduction quality of some of the logos and symbols in these appendices: they were photocopied from originals printed on a variety of plastic, card and other materials.

LOGOS (I)

1.

2.

OZONE FRIENDLY
CONTAINS NO FLUOROCARBONS

3.

4.

5. NO CFC

6.

CONTAINS NO PROPELLANT ALLEGED TO DAMAGE OZONE

7.

DOLPHIN FRIENDLY

8.

CFC FREE · OZONE FRIENDLY

9.

10.

11.

12. CFC FREE

13. ENVIRONMENT FRIENDLIER

OZONE SAFE

14.

15.

Not Tested on Animals

16.

HDPE

17.

ENVIRONMENT FRIENDLY
This product contains fluff pulp which is made with concern for the environment

18.

19.

100% RECYCLED RECYCLE

20.

PETE

21.

Jet

22.

100% RECYCLED PAPER

23.

GREEN CHECS

24.

25.

RESPECTING THE ENVIRONMENT 0% MERCURY/CADMIUM

26.

27.

DOLPHIN FRIENDLY

28.

RECYCLED

29.

DER GRÜNE PUNKT

30.

ENVIRONMENTAL INFORMATION

31.

THE BIO-D COMPANY

32.

ENVIRONMENTAL INFORMATION

33.

LOGOS (II)

34.

35.

36.

37.

38.

39.

40.

41.

CARING FOR THE ENVIRONMENT

42.

43.

44.

45.

46.

47.

48.

49.

50.

51.

Non-biol
Ultra
automati

52.

53.

54.

55.

RADION

ENVIRONMENTAL INFORMATION

Radion powder is produced to the highest standard in its formulation, packaging and manufacturing processes. All the ingredients are carefully selected and checked to safeguard you and your family.

BIODEGRADABLE To safeguard the environment the surface active ingredients of Radion are biodegradable and break down rapidly by natural processes into harmless substances.

ENERGY USAGE The oxygen based bleaching system ensures excellent performance at low temperatures, saving energy in heating the water.

PACKAGING The pack contains recycled cardboard materials and is recyclable.

PERSIL

ENVIRONMENT

► The surface active ingredients in Biological Persil liquid are biodegradable and breakdown rapidly into harmless substances.

► This carton uses half the packaging material of a 1L bottle. This carton is crushable for easy disposal.

BIO-D

Bio-D WASHING POWDER 1Kg e

THE BIO-D COMPANY

- **PRODUCTS FOR A CLEANER ENVIRONMENT**
- **PHOSPHATE FREE • ENZYME FREE**
- **PERFUME FREE • NO CHLORINE BLEACHES**
- **NO OPTICAL BRIGHTENERS**

Bio-D Washing Powder contains non-polluting zeolites as an alternative to phosphates. Detergents are fully biodegradable to a higher standard than required by EEC regulations.

BOLD

This Procter & Gamble product has been formulated and made with care for the environment. This care is shown in the rigorous selection and extensive checking of ingredients, packaging and manufacturing processes.

ENVIRONMENTAL INFORMATION

BIODEGRADABLE
The cleaning agents in this product are broken down by natural processes.

STAIN REMOVERS
This product contains gentle stain removers which remove stains by releasing active oxygen.

ENERGY USAGE
This formulation gives excellent performance at lower wash temperatures, saving energy in heating the wash water.

PACKAGING
This pack is made from 80% recycled material.

FABRIC SOFTENER
Bold's fabric softener is made from a naturally occurring ingredient.

GREEN CLEAN

Green Clean is kind to people and the environment.

All ingredients are completely biodegradable within 3-5 days. Using Green Clean as an alternative can help reduce pollution and thereby protect nature. Green Clean is 100% vegetarian and no animal testing is permitted.

No enzymes
No NTA or EDTA
No chlorine bleach
No optical brighteners
No synthetic perfumes
No phosphates/zeolites

DER GRÜNE PUNKT

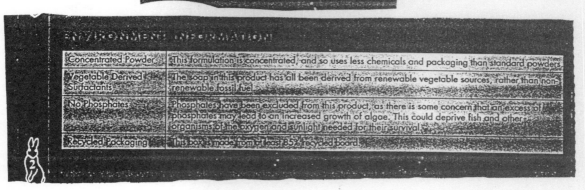

GREEN CHOICE

ENVIRONMENT INFORMATION	
Concentrated Powder	This formulation is concentrated, and so uses less chemicals and packaging than standard powders.
Vegetable Derived Surfactants	The soap in this product has all been derived from renewable vegetable sources, rather than non-renewable fossil fuel.
No Phosphates	Phosphates have been excluded from this product, as there is some concern that an excess of phosphates may lead to an increased growth of algae. This could deprive fish and other organisms of the oxygen and sunlight needed for their survival.
Recycled Packaging	This box is made from at least 85% recycled board.

ECOVER

ECOVER®
COMPANY INFORMATION

FROM A CARING COMPANY - ECOVER products are produced at the world's first ecological factory, a clean running plant that helps preserve the community while providing you with high quality products.

The UN elected ECOVER to the GLOBAL 500 Roll of Honour for outstanding environmental achievement.

FOR PEOPLE WHO CARE - ECOVER care about you and your environment and are committed to providing you with high performance products of high ecological value. ECOVER is against animal testing and uses alternative methods.
For advice or further information on the ECOVER range, write to:
ECOVER WASHING LINE, Woodburn Court, Burghclere, Berkshire RG15 9ED.

HIGHLY BIODEGRADABLE INGREDIENTS
This product is based only on highly effective minerals and plant based ingredients which biodegrade quickly with a minimum impact on the environment. Plant based surfactants (ionic and anionic tenside) lose all tensio-activity within 3-5 days (OECD Screening Test). Soap is fully biodegradable within 3 days (EMPA-Test).

Other products in the ECOVER washing range include :

ECOVER concentrated AUTOMATIC WASHING LIQUID,
ECOVER concentrated FABRIC CONDITIONER,
ECOVER concentrated WOOL WASH,
ECOVER LAUNDRY BLEACH and
ECOVER STAIN REMOVER.

ECOVER IS A REGISTERED TRADE MARK OF ECOVER NV.

85% recycled cardboard

5 412533 001808

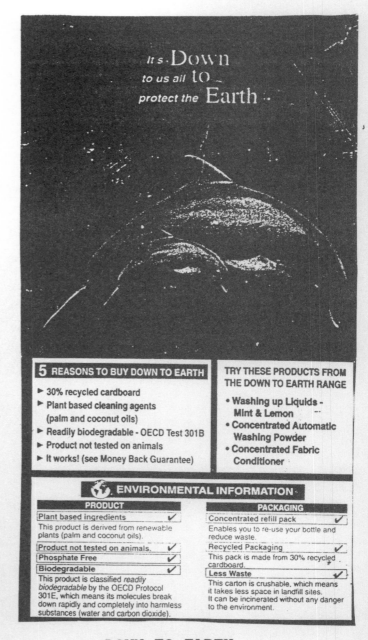

It's Down to us all to protect the Earth

5 REASONS TO BUY DOWN TO EARTH
► 30% recycled cardboard
► Plant based cleaning agents (palm and coconut oils)
► Readily biodegradable - OECD Test 301B
► Product not tested on animals
► It works! (see Money Back Guarantee)

TRY THESE PRODUCTS FROM THE DOWN TO EARTH RANGE
• Washing up Liquids - Mint & Lemon
• Concentrated Automatic Washing Powder
• Concentrated Fabric Conditioner

ENVIRONMENTAL INFORMATION

PRODUCT		PACKAGING	
Plant based ingredients	✓	Concentrated refill pack	✓
This product is derived from renewable plants (palm and coconut oils).		Enables you to re-use your bottle and reduce waste.	
Product not tested on animals.	✓	Recycled Packaging	✓
Phosphate Free	✓	This pack is made from 30% recycled cardboard.	
Biodegradable	✓	Less Waste	✓
This product is classified *readily biodegradable* by the OECD Protocol 301E, which means its molecules break down rapidly and completely into harmless substances (water and carbon dioxide).		This carton is crushable, which means it takes less space in landfill sites. It can be incinerated without any danger to the environment.	

DOWN TO EARTH

CAN RECYCLED REALLY BE THIS *Soft?*

Softer ON THE ENVIRONMENT, TOO...

SOFTER ON THE ENVIRONMENT

MADE FROM 100% RECYCLED PAPER

Nouvelle has always been the bench-mark in quality for brands made from 100% recycled paper.

Not only do you save trees when you buy *New Improved Nouvelle* - you also save water. This is because our manufacturing processes are amongst the most advanced and resource-efficient in the world.

NOUVELLE

Made from 100% Low Grade Waste

ENVIRONMENT FRIENDLIE

Sainsbury's Greencare Toilet Tissue is manufactured from 100% low grade waste paper.
80% of this is recycled newspaper and 20% is recycled magazines.
Most of this waste would otherwise have been buried or incinerated.

SAINSBURY'S GREENCARE

WHEN YOU BUY SAINSBURY'S REVIVE

YOU ARE HELPING TO MAKE A MORE

EFFECTIVE USE OF NATURAL RESOURCES

BECAUSE REVIVE IS MANUFACTURED

FROM

100% RECYCLED PAPER

SAINSBURY'S REVIVE

 Thank you for choosing our new bathroom tissue. Now DIXCEL offers you a product which is made entirely without the use of chlorine bleaching.

 Chlorine has been traditionally used to help meet the high standards of brightness, strength and cleanliness expected by you the customer. However, our technology now enables us to meet these standards with a TOTALLY CHLORINE FREE bleaching process.

 As with the manufacture of all DIXCEL products no wood pulp from tropical rainforests is ever used and we do not add optical brightening agents.

Best of all DIXCEL Non-Chlorine Bleached bathroom tissue offers you the choice of a quality tissue at an everyday good price, whilst helping to protect our environment.

This new product from DIXCEL gives you the choice of a Non-Chlorine Bleached bathroom tissue alongside our KittenSoft luxury soft range and Family Value recycled products.

DIXCEL

SUMA

HARVEST

The Expanding Forests

Pine for Corndell is harvested in the huge forests of Sweden and Finland. And to replace every tree that is felled for Corndell, foresters are obliged to plant several new seedling trees. The result? There are more standing trees in those countries to-day than at any time since the last ice age.

Pine from these Scandinavian trees is beautifully figured, close grained, and ideal for the best cabinet work.

CORNDELL FURNITURE

Young trees in early growth.

Safeguarding the environment.

CARE FOR THE ENVIRONMENT

It is not only the timber that undergoes a strict process of selection. The forests themselves are specially chosen for their programmes of replanting and renewal. For every tree felled we ensure that at least four new trees are planted, thus safeguarding the environment and the supply of timber for future generations.

DUCAL FURNITURE

About this book...

The paper used in the printing of this brochure has been rated under the "Eco-check" system, a method of monitoring the environmental acceptability of paper products that has been introduced by R.A. Brand and Company Limited in advance of projected legislation on the subject.

Under the Eco-check system, papers and paper mills are examined under five separate criteria: fibre source sustainability (ensuring that the pulp has been taken from renewable, managed forest resources); energy source and efficiency of the production process; minimising of chlorinated organics, including dioxins, in the production process; liquid effluent and solid waste levels from the paper mill; and finally gaseous emissions from the mill. For each section that meets the required standard, the Eco-check system awards one star, with five being the maximum.

This book has been printed on Grandeur Web Matt, a paper awarded a 5-star Eco-check rating through specification with Brands Papers.

ERCOL FURNITURE

WEEDKILLERS

WEEDOL

BIO

ROUNDUP

WEED MASTER

SPEEDWEED

TUMBLEWEED

<u>GARDEN COMPOST</u>

NEW HORIZON by J.ARTHUR BOWERS'

PEAT-FREE MULTIPURPOSE COMPOST

"AN ENVIRONMENTALLY FRIENDLY PRODUCT"

BIO MULTI COMPOST

Peat-Free Bio Multicompost No.1

B&Q HOUSEPLANT COMPOST

PEAT CONTAINED IN THIS
PRODUCT HAS NOT BEEN
HARVESTED FROM AREAS
OF SCIENTIFIC INTEREST

GAROTTA COMPOST MAKER

OCEAN

ECO SPRAY WASHING MACHINES

ECO SPRAY WASH SYSTEM

The washers use a paddle lift and spray action which by constantly keeping the water moving around the drum, greatly reduces water and energy consumption.

Every machine has OCEAN's Rinse and Hold facility which suspends delicate and synthetic fabrics in the last rinse water, preventing them from becoming creased during the final spin.

MIELE

Forgive us for blowing our trumpet again, but the long life of a Miele machine is now legendary. It is our belief, however, that if an appliance is to last way into the future, there should be a future for it to be around in.

So, towards an even cleaner future (and washday), we have developed a detergent saving system that will prove as economical to you as it is friendly to the environment. And like all brilliant ideas, it is brilliantly simple. While you save on detergent, the environment enjoys the minimum pollution of waste water.

CARING FOR THE
ENVIRONMENT

Such environmental and energy saving considerations have long been a tradition with us. Even our earliest models, dating back as far as 1925, were designed with energy efficiency in mind.

BOSCH

Our commitment to the environment.

al to the Bosch corporate phil-
ny is its commitment to develop-
omestic appliances designed to
de the greatest possible protec-
gainst pollution and waste while
erforming their functions with
eatest possible efficiency and
omy.

We use environmentally-friendly
materials and manufacturing processes and make the same high de-
mands of our suppliers. Recyclable
components, e.g. plastics are clearly
marked as such.

**Washing machines that harness
our natural resources:**

AEG

AEG's 'Cradle-to-Grave' environmental policy

True commitment to ecological concerns cannot begin and end with the production line. AEG therefore operates a 'Cradle-to-Grave' policy to ensure that environmental issues are paramount through every stage of an appliance's life.

By choosing an AEG domestic appliance, you may be sure that you are buying a product of the most thorough research into all aspects of environmental concern.

Environmental details on design, manufacturing, packaging, performance and recycling follow.
. . . .

HOOVER

HOOVER is committed to Environmental Protection

HOOVER is doing more for the environment. By changing our production technologies, we at HOOVER start environmental protection right from the manufacturing stage.

For example in selecting the materials used: HOOVER washing machine production only uses HCFC-free materials and non-toxic dyes. Wherever possible consumables and replaceable parts are made from recyclable materials. HOOVER production factories are equiped with the latest energy and water saving plants and water preparation equipment, to ensure that the manufacturing process is as kind on the environment as possible. What's more HOOVER washing machines are despatched exclusively using recyclable packing materials.

HOOVER – working for the future of each and every one of us.

The Ecolabel – Environmental supreme accolade

This is the Ecolabel. You'll be seeing it on more and more products as time goes by. But when it comes to washing machines you'll be seeing it first and foremost EXCLUSIVELY on the HOOVER New Wave. It has a simple, essential message to proclaim about the product on which it appears:

This Product is the most environmentally friendly in its Class!
Another 1st for HOOVER and it's not HOOVER saying it – it's the European Community Commission in Brussels. Why should they get involved? Because so many confusing – even misleading – claims are made by manufactures of all kinds of appliances that the Council of Environment Ministers set up an independent, authoritative set of environmental performance criteria which would indicate clearly and unmistakably which products are less environmentally damaging than others in the same class. The Ecolabel scheme has all the force of E.C. law.

Europe's first Ecolabel. And HOOVER New Wave scoops it!
There will eventually be other Ecolabels on all types of everyday products. But there's only one "first"; it was washing machines, and HOOVER have it in New Wave. The winning combination within the New Wave design that gave HOOVER this unique "first" was the **Eco Wash System Plus** and **Dynamic Spin Rinsing** system, since it romped home against SEVEN vital criteria.

AEG's 'Cradle-to-Grave' environmental policy

True commitment to ecological concerns cannot begin and end with the production line. AEG therefore operates a 'Cradle-to-Grave' policy to ensure that environmental issues are paramount through every stage of an appliance's life.

Design

The initial research and development process is the most important aspect of making an environmentally benign product.

Thoughtful production design and the use of the latest technology allows AEG to manufacture appliances using fewer types and smaller quantities of raw materials and to facilitate extraction of any reusable components at the end of the appliance's life.

Manufacturing

During manufacture 'waste' is kept to a minimum and is sorted and recycled wherever possible.

Packaging

Even AEG's choice of packaging material takes account of the ecological balance by using plastics which can either be burned without the production of toxic emission or recycled.

Performance

AEG appliances are amongst the most efficient available today. All have extremely low consumption values in terms of electricity and, where applicable, water and detergent. These savings, spread over the life of the appliance, make a significant contribution not only to your purse, but towards helping care for the environment and preserve natural resources.

Recycling

Whilst it is most important to optimise performance, it is also important to ensure that as many components as possible are easily separable and recyclable when the appliance is disposed of.

AEG has, for example, ensured that all electrical wiring looms (containing copper wire) can be simply unclipped for easy and cost effective recycling. Electric motors and other major components are held in place with the minimum of fastenings for the same reason.

In addition, all plastic components are coded to simplify eventual sorting and recycling by type of plastic.

By choosing an AEG domestic appliance, you may be sure that you are buying a product of the most thorough research into all aspects of environmental concern.

WHIRLPOOL

Whirlpool is totally committed to the protection of the environment and has eliminated CFC's from its 1995 production. The latest technology and the use of new compounds have ensured that Whirlpool appliances will continue to perform efficiently and at the same time present NO RISK of damage to the ozone layer.

MIELE

LIEBHERR

"Liebherr was the first to adapt its entire range of products to operate without CFCs in the foam insulation and in the refrigerant circuit. The insulation foamed with hydrocarbons is also free of fluorinated hydrocarbons.(..) With non polluting coating processes without the use of solvents, the identification of all plastics and the exclusive utilisation of recyclable materials Liebherr makes a further active contribution to the protection of our environment.

TRICITY BENDIX

THE ENVIRONMENT

In 1989 Tricity Bendix was the first UK manufacturer to introduce 50% reduced C.F.C. insulation. Now with thicker insulation and better seals, the refrigerant in the Cooling System has been reduced by 10-40% – no other manufacturer can match this! Also improved efficiency means less electricity is used and thus less fossil fuels are burnt, contributing to reducing the 'green house effect'.

These, along with many of the other benefits, make Tricity Bendix the only choice for the 1990's. And with such a range of appliances, choice will be your only problem.

ZANUSSI

FREEZONE COOLING - CFC FREE

Care of our environment is an ongoing commitment at Zanussi. Freezone cooling means all our appliances are totally CFC free.

Replacements for CFCs in both the refrigerant and the foam give optimum cooling performance and help ensure there is no negative effect on the ozone layer

Appendix 3

Symbols and logos: packaging

APPENDIX 3 Packaging Symbols

1

1 PETE	Polyethylene Terephthalate	5 PP	Polypropylene
2 HDPE	High Density Polyethylene	6 PS	Polystyrene
3 V	PVC	7 OTHER	All other resins and multi-materials
4 LDPE	Low Density Polyethylene		

The SPI System

2

3

4

Packaging made partly or entirely of recycled material:

X% = percentage of recycled material used in the manufacturing of the product

Reusable packaging:

Recyclable packaging:

Appendix 4

Symbols and logos: timber and food

APPENDIX 4

Logos and Symbols found on timber and food

Timber

APPENDIX 4

Logos and Symbols found on timber and food

Food

Biodynamic Agricultural
Association

Irish Organic Farmers and
Growers Association

Organic Farmers and
Growers

Organic Food Federation

Scottish Organic Producers
Association

Soil Association Organic
Marketing Company

Conservation Grade

Appendix 5

The British codes of advertising and sales promotion code on environmental claims

1. The basis of any claim should be explained clearly and should be qualified where necessary. Unqualified claims can mislead if they omit significant information.

2. Claims such as 'environmental friendly' or 'wholly biodegradable' should not be used without qualification unless advertisers can provide convincing evidence that their product will cause no environmental damage. Qualified claims and comparisons such as 'greener' or 'friendlier' may be acceptable if advertisers can substantiate that their product provides an overall improvement in environmental terms either against their competitors' or their own previous products.

3. Where there is a significant division of scientific opinion or where evidence is in conclusive this should be reflected in any statements made in the advertisement. Advertisers should not suggest that their claims command universal acceptance if it is not the case.

4. If a product has never had a demonstrably adverse effect on the environment, advertisements should not imply that the formulation has changed to make it safe. It is legitimate, however, to make claims about a product whose composition has changed or has always been designed in a way that omits chemicals known to cause damage to the environment.

5. The use of extravagant language should be avoided, as should bogus and confusing scientific terms. If it is necessary to use a scientific expression, its meaning should be clear.

Appendix 6

International Chamber of Commerce Code on environmental advertising

The ICC International Code of Advertising Practice is widely accepted as the basis for promoting high standards of ethics in advertising, by self-regulation against a background of national and international law. The Code recognises social responsibilities towards the consumer and the community, and is designed primarily as an instrument for self-discipline.

Because of the growing importance of environmental issues and the complexity of judging and verifying environmental claims, the ICC has decided to produce an Environmental Advertising Code, in order to extend the area of self-discipline and to help business to make responsible use of environmental advertising. National rules and guidelines, where applicable, have been taken into account, as well as the ICC's Business Charter for Sustainable Development, together with the ICC position paper on Environmental Labelling Schemes.

Definitions in environmental terminology have not crystallised yet and vary currently between countries, and between industrial sectors. Consequently, specific definitions are not included in the Code, but further work within the ICC may make it possible to recommend such definitions in a future edition which should then be incorporated into the international Code of Advertising Practice.

Scope of the Code

This Code applies to all advertisements containing environmental claims, in all media. It thus covers any form of advertising in which explicit or implicit reference is made to environmental or ecological aspects relating to the production, packaging, distribution, use/consumption or disposal of goods, services or facilities (collectively termed products). All are covered by the Code.

This Code should be seen as an extension of the ICC Code of Advertising Practice which therefore remains applicable on any aspect not specifically dealt with in this Code. The Code on Environmental Advertising should also be read in conjunction with the other ICC Codes of Marketing Practice, namely

- Marketing Research Practice
- Sales Promotion Practice
- Direct Marketing Practice
- Direct Sales Practice

Interpretation

The Code is to be applied in the spirit as well as in the letter.

Basic principles

All environmental advertising should be legal, decent, honest and truthful. It should be consistent with environmental regulations and mandatory programmes and should conform to the principles of fair competition, as generally accepted in business.

No advertisements or claims should be such as to impair public confidence in the efforts made by the business community to improve its ecological performance.

Rules

Honesty
Article 1
Advertisements should be so framed as not to abuse consumers' concern for the environment, or exploit their possible lack of environmental knowledge.

Environmental behaviour
Article 2
Advertisements should not appear to approve or encourage actions which contravene the law, self-regulating codes or generally accepted standards of environmentally responsible behaviour.

Truthful presentation
Article 3
Advertisements should not contain any statement or presentation likely to mislead consumers in any way about the environmental aspects or advantages of products, or about the actions being taken by the advertiser in favour of the environment. Corporate advertisements can refer to specific products or actions, but not imply without justification that they extend to the whole performance or a company, group or industry. Expressions such as 'environmentally friendly' or 'ecologically safe' implying that a product or activity has no impact - or only a positive impact - on the environment should not be used unless a very high standard of proof is available.

Scientific research

Article 4

Advertisements should only use technical demonstrations or scientific findings about environmental impact, when backed by serious scientific work.

Environmental jargon or scientific terminology is acceptable provided it is relevant and used in a way that can be readily understood by consumers.

Testimonials

Article 5

In view of the rapid developments in environmental science and technology, particular care should be taken to ensure that, when testimonials or endorsements are used to support an environmental claim in an advertisement, changes in product formulation or market circumstances have not made the testimonial out of date.

Superiority

Article 6

Environmental superiority over competitors can only be claimed when a significant advantage can be demonstrated. Claims in relation to competitive products, when based on the absence of a harmful ingredient or a damaging effect, are only acceptable when other products in the category do include the ingredient or cause the effect.

Product ingredients and elements

Article 7

Environmental claims should not imply that they relate to more stages of a product-life cycle, or to more properties of a product, than justified and should where necessary clearly indicate to which stage or which property they refer.

When advertisements refer to the reduction of ingredients or elements having a negative environmental impact, it must be clear what has been reduced. Alternative elements, if any, must bring a significant ecological improvement.

Signs and symbols

Article 8

Environmental signs or symbols should only be used in an advertisement when the source of these signs or symbols is clearly indicated, and there is no confusion over the meaning. Such signs and symbols should not falsely suggest official approval.

Waste collection recycling and disposal

Article 9

Environmental claims referring to waste separation, collection, processing or disposal are acceptable provided that the recommended method or collection, processing or disposal is generally accepted or sufficiently available, or the extent or availability is accurately described.

Substantiation

Article 10

Descriptions, claims or illustrations relating to verifiable facts should be capable of substantiation. Advertisers should have such substantiation available so that they can produce evidence without delay to the self-regulatory bodies responsible for the operation of the International Code of Advertising Practice.

Appendix 7

The terms of the government's review

Review of controls over trade descriptions and statements which include environmental claims for consumer goods and services

Project to be conducted by the National Consumer Council

Background

1. During the late 1980s there was a growing awareness in the UK of the impact which consumer products have on the environment. Consumers became increasingly interested in brands of product which appeared to be less environmentally harmful than others. Many manufacturers responded to this interest by venturing information, in their advertising or product labelling, about the environmental performance of their products.

2. However, concerns began to be expressed to the Government that in some cases the claims made by manufacturers and retailers were confusing or misleading. This led to concern, shared by some Trading Standards Officers, that the main existing legislation dealing with the misdescription of products (the Trade Descriptions Act 1968 - or 'TDA') might not be able to deal with false and misleading environmental claims, as it does not refer specifically, in the definition of those matters which can constitute a trade description, to the environmental characteristics of products.

3.   The Government responded to these concerns with the following statement in the 1990 Environment White Paper:

The Government intends, when Parliamentary time is available, to legislate to tighten the provisions of the Trade Descriptions Act 1968 as regards environmental claims. The main aim is to put beyond any doubt that the Act covers environmental claims, and to require those making claims to produce evidence to substantiate those claims if challenged. (Cm 1200, p. 222.)

4.   The Government has subsequently been questioned about this expression of intent by members of the public, consumer groups and businesses, as well as by the Environment Select Committee. And in the 1993/94 session of Parliament Alan Keen MP introduced (though unsuccessfully) a Private Member's Bill - the Environmental Claims Bill - which aimed to legislate against false or misleading environmental claims.

5.   The Government remains committed to the basis principle of ensuring effective protection for consumers. But it has become clear that the position is not as straightforward as was assumed when the 1990 White Paper was written.

●   There have been some successful prosecutions under the TDA in the area of environmental claims - suggesting that the existing legislation offers more scope for dealing with the problem than previously thought.

●   It is therefore questionable whether some of the legislative changes which have been proposed would offer any more protection to the consumer than the existing TDA regime.

- Lawyers have also identified significant difficulties with some of the legislative solutions proposed (eg., problems with reversing the normal legal principles for proving an offence, and with attempting to outlaw the use of particular phrases).

- The problem of claims which are made in very generalised terms may be one that cannot ultimately be dealt with effectively through specific legislation.

6. The Department of the Environment (DOE) and the Department of Trade and Industry (DTI) have therefore asked the National Consumer Council to examine the current position and to report to Ministers, with a view to establishing, where necessary, practical ways forward to deliver the basic aim of ensuring effective protection for consumers.

Outline of the review

7. The main aims of the proposed review are:

A. To establish the extent to which consumers are affected by false or misleading environmental claims or statements about goods or services and the extent to which those claims and statements are covered by current controls - both statutory controls (in particular the provisions of the Trade Descriptions Act 1968) and non-statutory.

B. To identify any areas where the current controls do not provide effective protection to consumers against such claims or statements, or where there is uncertainty as to the extent to which they are covered.

C. To provide the basis for a clear statement of guidance on the coverage of the existing controls.

D. To make recommendations for action (whether involving legislative or non-statutory measures) to deal effectively with any areas where false or misleading claims or statements are not covered, or where their coverage is uncertain.

8. The review will be concerned only with claims made about the environmental impact of products or services in the course of their life cycle. It will not deal with other issues which might be raised about products - relating, for example, to a manufacturer's policy on ethical or welfare issues (such as the testing of products on animals).

9. Food, drink and pharmaceutical products, though within the scope of the TDA, are covered by detailed regimes on labelling and advertising which are the responsibility of other Government departments. The present review is only concerned with these product areas to the extent of any claims which might be made about the environmental impact of particular products.

Further details of the work required

10. In order to fulfil the aims of the review, the following steps will need to be included in the programme of the work.

A. To establish the extent to which consumers are affected by false or misleading environmental claims or statements about goods or service and the extent to which those claims and statements are covered by current controls - both statutory controls (in particular the provisions of the Trade Descriptions Act 1968) and non-statutory.

i   Examine the current state of practice with a sample of Trading Standards Officers, via the Local Authority Co-ordinating Body on Food and Trading Standards (LACOTS).

ii   Examine the coverage of the 1968 Act in relation to different types of environmental claim.

iii Examine significant cases where prosecutions have been brought by Trading Standards Officers for false or misleading environmental claims.

iv   Take account of relevant reports and documents relating to statutory and non statutory controls, including:

- the 1994 report by the London Borough of Sutton ('An evaluation of the use of environmental claims in marketing in the United Kingdom');

- the guidelines and any relevant research on environmental claims in advertising codes (including those produced by the Advertising Standards Authority, the Independent Television Commission, and the Radio Authority);

- the Guidelines for Non Advertising Green Claims issued by DTI;

- the International Standards Organisation draft report on Self Declaration Environmental claims (ISO / TC 207 /SC 3);

- the provisions of the EC ecolabelling scheme, which is being implemented in the UK by the United Kingdom Ecolabelling Board.

v Consult with:

- DTI's legal advisers;
- the Office of Fair Trading;
- the United Kingdom Ecolabelling Board;
- relevant experts in advertising and retailing;
- relvant consumer and environmental groups;
- the sponsors of the Environmental Claims Bill.

vi Establish consumers' experience and understanding of these types of claims and statements, and the effect on consumers purchasing behaviour and use of the relevant product or service. The methodology will depend on existing available consumer research in this field and could include market research.

B. To identify any areas where the current controls do not provide effective protection to consumers against such claims or statements, or where there is uncertainty as to the extent to which they are covered.

i Specify the different types of environmental claim which appear not to be susceptible to control under the terms of the existing regimes.

ii Assess the significance of such claims and the benefits to be gained if more effective control could be achieved.

iii Identify the particular areas where it can be shown that improvements in control might produce significant, quantified benefits.

C. To provide the basis for a clear statement of guidance on the coverage of the existing controls.

i Draw together the findings under A and B above into an authoritative account of how the existing forms of control can be applied to different types of environmental claim.

ii Summarise these findings in a way that could be readily turned into guidance for Trading Standards Officers, manufacturers, retailers and consumers.

D. To make recommendations for action (whether involving legislative or non-statutory measures) to deal effectively with any areas where false or misleading claims or statements are not covered, or where their coverage is uncertain.

i Assess whether any improvements considered necessary could be achieved more effectively by legislative means or by voluntary arrangements (eg., through codes of practice for manufacturers, retailers or advertisers).

ii Consult DTI legal advertisers on any recommendations which would involve amending or adding to existing statutory provisions, and take into account their advice on the principles and practicalities of any changes to the existing regime in UK law and of the relationship with other areas of UK and European law.

iii Identify in the recommendations:

- the public expenditure costs (including those of enforcement authorities) of implementing each proposal;

- any significant additional costs or burdens falling on private enterprise (including small businesses).

Appendix 8

The organisations we consulted

Mr Andrew Brown *
Advertising Association
London

Ms Matti Alderson *
Advertising Standards Authority
London

Advice Services Alliance
London

Mr Carl Rawlings *
Alliance for Beverage
  Cartons & the Environment
Newcastle-Upon-Tyne

Ms Jane Vaus
Ark Environmental Foundation
London

Mr Gordon Madden
ASDA
Leeds

Ms Linda Taylor
Association for the
  Conservation of Energy
London

---

* indicates a response

David Vernon *
Australian Consumers' Council
Australia

Mr Alan Knight *
B&Q plc
Hants

Birmingham Consumers' Group
Birmingham

Birmingham Consumers Advice
  Centre
Birmingham

Mr David Wheeler *
The Body Shop Intl plc
Littlehampton

Mr H Gay
The Legal Department
The Boots Co. plc
Nottingham

Mr Robin Simpson *
Brewers & Licensed Retailers
  Association
London

Mr David Roberts *
British Aerosol Manufacturers'
  Association
London

The Director
British Plastics Federation
London

Mr Michael Bellingham *
British Retail Consortium
London

British Standards Institution
    Consumer Policy Committee
London

Mr Geoffrey Draughn *
Broadcast Advertising
    Clearance Centre
London

Mr Vincent Perrot
Bureau Europeen des Unions de
    Consummateurs (BEUC) *
Belgium

Mr Edwin Datchefski *
The Business and Environment
    Consultancy
London

Mr D R Fry *
Carter Wallace Ltd
Folkestone

Mr Robert Housman
Centre for International
    Environmental Law
USA

Prof. Robin Grove White *
Centre for Study of Environmental
    Change
Lancaster University
Lancaster

Citizens Advice Scotland *
Edinburgh

Prof. Fell *
Commonwealth Trade Practices
    Commission
Australia

Mr J Cridland
Confederation of British Industry
London

Mr Franz Fiala
Consumer Council of the
    Austrian Standards Institute
Austria

Ms Sheila McKechnie
Consumers Association
London

Mr Steven Crampton *
Consumers in Europe Group
London

Philip Evans *
Consumers International
London

Mr Ed Groth *
Consumers Union
USA

Ms Jenny Hillard
Consumers' Association of
   Canada
Canada

D L Wilkinson
Co-operative Union
Manchester

Mr Bill Shannon   *
Co-operative Wholesale Society
Manchester

Ms Marion Kelly   *
The Cosmetic Toiletry &
   Perfumery Association
London

Ms Fiona Reynolds   *
Council for the Protection of
   Rural England
London

Mr P Cooper
Courtaulds Textiles
Nottingham

Mr Peter Webster   *
EIRIS
London

Mr Simon Whalley
Environmental Counselling
   & Communications
Devizes

Ethical Consumer Research
   Association
Manchester

Karola Taschner
European Environmental Bureau
Belgium

Federation of Independent
   Advice Centres
London

Ms Rose-Marie Schneebergen
Fédération Nationale
Associations de Consommateurs du
   Quebec
Canada

Mr M A Hunt   *
Food and Drink Federation
London

Friends of the Earth Scotland
Edinburgh

Mr Charles Secrett
Friends of the Earth
London

Ms Maeve Bell   *
General Consumer Council
   for Northern Ireland
Belfast

Prof. Graham Ashworth
Going for Green
C/o Tidy Britain Group
Wigan

Mr Steve Crewe
Great Mills (Retail) Ltd
Bristol

Ms Julie Hill   *

Green Alliance
London

Lord Melchett *
Greenpeace UK
London

Dr Dick Robson
ICI
London

Mr John Hooper *
Incorporated Society of
  British Advertisers
London

Mr Frank Willis *
Independent Television
  Commission
London

Ms Jane Bickerstaffe *
Industry Council for Packaging &
    the Environment (INCPEN)
London

Mr David Wilkinson
Institute for European
  Environmental Policy
London

Institute of Consumers Affairs
c/o Mid-Glamorgan
Trading Standards Department
Pontyprydd

Mr Philip Circus *
Institute of Practitioners in
  Advertising
London

Institute of Trading Standards
  Administration
Hadleigh

Mr Julian Lewis
International Institute for
  the Environment & Development
London

Mr Neil Robson *
ITC
Geneva

Mr Sander van Bennekom *
IUCN World Conservation Union

Mr Keith Hale *
Local Authorities Co-ordinating
  Body on Food and Trading
Standards
Croydon

Law Centres Federation
London

Leicester Consumer Advice Centre
Leicester

Mr Ian Randall *
Marks & Spencer plc
London

Mr R S Davis
Metal Packaging Manufacturers'
  Association
Slough

Mr Philip Cunningham
MFI
London

Ms Siv Naslund *
Ministry of the Environment
Sweden

National Association of *
  Citizens Advice Bureaux
London

Mr Bob Gale *
National Federation of Consumer
  Groups
Newcastle-Upon-Tyne

National Federation of Women's
  Institutes *
London

Neighbourhood Energy Action
Newcastle-upon-Tyne

Mr Richard Adams
New Consumer
Newcastle-Upon-Tyne

Mr Tim Cooper *
The New Economics Foundation
London

Mr Tormond Lien *
Norwegian Foundation for
E   nvironmental Labelling
Norway

Ms Rebecca Hanmer *
Pollution Division
OECD
France

Ms Cathy Bradley *
PAPERBACK Campaign
Swindon

Ms Chrissie Maher
Plain English Campaign
Stockport

Ms Samantha Hill *
Consumer Affairs Division
Office of Fair Trading
London

Plymouth Consumer Group
Plymouth

Mrs Pippa Hyam
Projects in Partnership
London

Mr Colin Thompson
Public Relations Consultants Assoc.
London

Mr Tony Stoller *
The Radio Authority
London

Research Institute for Consumer
   Affairs
London

Ms Nicola Ellen *
Safeway
Hayes

Ms Alison Austin *
J Sainsbury plc
London S

Scottish Consumer Council *
Glasgow

Mr Gary Parker *
SmithKline Beecham
Research Technology Service
Centre
Weybridge

Mr Keith Chesterton *
The Soap and Detergent
   Industry Association
Hayes

Mr Patrick Holden *
The Soil Association
Bristol

Ms Julia Hales
SustainAbility
London

Ms Agneta Melin *
Swedish Environmental
   Protection Agency
Dept. of Energy, Transport
Waste and Management
Sweden
Mr Christoph Juen *

Swiss Federation of
   Commerce and Industry
Switzerland

Tannochside Information and
   Advice Centre
Uddingston

Mr John Longworth *
Tesco Stores Ltd
Cheshunt

Ms Gail Gunn *
Tetra Pak UK
Uxbridge

Townswomens' Guilds *
Chamber of Commerce House
Birmingham

Mr Jerry Rendell *
UK Ecolabelling Board
London

Mr David R Cope *
The UK Centre for Economic
   and Environmental Development
Cambridge

US Federal Trade Commission *
6th Street and Pennsylvania Avenue
USA

Mr Tim Watkins *
Welsh Consumer Council
Cardiff

Ms Angela Mawle
Women's Environmental Network
London

Mr P Parker
Woolworths plc
London

Dr Robin Pellew
WWF
Godalming

Mike Read *
Consultant to WWF UK
Salisbury

**Other replies received
via the General Consumer Council
for Northern Ireland**

Mr W B Oliphant *
Western Group Environmental
Health Committee
Omagh District Council
Omagh

Mr William Francey *
Health & Environmental Services
  Department
Belfast City Council
Belfast

Mr R J Johnston *
Trading Standards Branch
Belfast

Mr Michael Joyce *
Southern Group Public Health
Committee
Constituent Councils: Armagh,
Banbridge, Craigavon, Dungannon,
Newry and Mourne
Armagh

Mr J Patterson *
Eastern Group Public Health
Committee
Castlereagh Borough Council
Co. Down

Green claims

Other National Consumer Council publications

We publish a wide range of other policy papers, reports and handbooks on current consumer issues. These are just a few of our recent titles. To find out more about NCC books, please phone us on **0171 730 3469**.

Charging Consumers for Social Services A major review of local authority policy and practice, 1995, 164 pages, £11.50

Financial Services and Low-income Consumers How less well-off consumers perceive bank and building society services, 1995, 46 pages, £7.50

Seeking Civil Justice A unique investigation into people's experiences when they become involved in a legal dispute, 1995, 118 pages, £14.50

Consumer Concerns 1995 A national opinion survey on local council services, 1995, 56 pages, £10

Problems for Pedestrians A national opinion survey, 1995, 32 pages, £10

In Partnership with Patients Involving the community in general practice - a handbook for GPs and practice staff, 1995, 24 pages, £5

Agricultural Policy in the European Union The consumer agenda for reform, 1995, 104 pages, £12

Competition and Consumers Policy and practice in the UK today, 1995, 94 pages, £12

Consulting Your Consumers A handbook for public service managers, 1994, 48 pages, £8.50

These prices include postage and packing.

To order any of these books, please write to:
NCC Publications, 20 Grosvenor Gardens, London SW1W ODH

Please send a cheque with your order, payable to: National Consumer Council.

On the previous page is a list of recent National Consumer Council publications. We can often arrange for you to have our print publications in another format, like braille, audio-tape, computer disk (in WordPerfect) or large print. Please contact us for more information.

National Consumer Council, 20 Grosvenor Gardens, London SW1W ODH
Telephone 0171 730 3469
Fax 0171 730 0191
Minicom 0171 730 3469